NO LONGER PROFITABLE.

THE LEAVEN IN A GREAT CITY

By LILLIAN W. BETTS

I L L U S T R A T E D

NEW YORK
DODD, MEAD & COMPANY
1902

First Edition published September, 1902.

CONTENTS

LIST OF ILLUSTRATIONS

CHAPTER I.

AT THE BOTTOM.

ONE of the first, and, up to the present time, one of the most interesting experiments made in New York for the better housing of the poor, was made in the early eighties by a score or less of philanthropic capitalists. These gentlemen organized a stock company to hold and manage tenement-house property, limiting their dividends to three per cent. on the capital; the surplus dividends, if any, over this amount, to be used in improving the property, and securing such conditions and opportunities for the tenants as would stimulate pride and independence. The formation of this company followed one of the periodic agitations of the tenement-house problems customary in New York.

In 1878 a conference was called by the State Charities' Aid Association to consider the condition of the tenement houses in this city. Mr. Alfred T. White, of Brooklyn, had at this time proved that model tenements, conducted on strictly business principles, paid as investments, and stated at this conference that his model houses made a return of seven one-half per cent. As a result of this conference a committee was appointed who reported that they did not find it desirable to recommend the building of model tenements in New York at this time. Mr. White for many years stood alone as the man of wealth with the courage of his convictions, that there were wage-earners compelled to live under tenement-house conditions who would pay for and respect the best housing that capital would offer them, within their rent-paying capacity.

The tenement-house agitation continued

In 1879 Mayor Cooper had appointed a committee known as the "Mayor's Committee," to devise means to effect tenement-house reforms. This committee reported, and among other suggestions recommended, that companies be organized to build modern tenements. Some members of this committee, with others, formed the stock company alluded to with a capital of $300,000. With a wisdom peculiarly their own, they did not wait until model buildings could be erected according to plans not yet drawn on sites not yet selected, but they leased on a long lease property that had been unproductive for a long time, and occupied by a people at the lowest level of the home-making people of the city. Below them are the people who do not even pretend to make a home. This property was located in the old Fourth Ward. It was the reputation of this ward, and the record of the particular property, which doubtless led these capitalists to secure it. It was conceded that the poverty and degradation of the Fourth Ward was at least as great as in any other section of the city. The property leased had attracted public attention and been the subject of special investigation and reports in every agitation of the tenement-house problem since 1856.

The Fourth Ward criminal and health records figure for an even longer period in every effort at bettering municipal conditions by the example it presented of civic indifference, neglect and maladministration. The houses faced on two alleys, known in their best days as "Single" and "Double" alley, respectively. As this distinction indicates, on Single Alley one row of houses faced the walls of the adjoining property, while two rows of houses faced each other across Double Alley. Later known as Swipe's Alley, Guzzle Row, Hell's Kitchen, Murderers' Row, showing the gradual descent from respectability. There is a tradition that Single Alley once had gardens that extended to Roosevelt Street; that the houses had been occupied by one family; but this cannot be verified. In their most degenerate days these houses had an air of exclusiveness, due doubtless to their fronting on courts and the tall iron fences, with gates, that separated the houses from the street. The neighborhood at one time was aristocratic; Franklin Square, but a short distance from the property, was a social center of national greatness. As business went northward, the merchants, bankers, tradespeople, followed, for the tie between home and business was still very close; the midday dinner made distance between the two impossible. The old homes were left for subdivision among the skilled workmen and clerks.

The tide of immigration set in, and the strangers settled near the docks and wharfs—the source of their wages; in time they crowded into the old residences, beginning the housing problem of New York. These old homes were soon overcrowded. They could not be made sanitary. The demand for room was so great that the large closets—the necessity of the old-time housekeepers—were counted bedrooms, and are to-day in houses of this type in tenement-house regions throughout the city.

The property secured by the new company at the time it was leased was a part of a large estate, the owner of which during his lifetime had personally cared for it. He was both strict and just, and these two attributes preserved these houses for years after the property in the neighborhood had begun to yield to the character of later residents. This owner kept the alleys and the houses in repair. The semi-privacy the iron gate gave the tenants was for years the reason that the better-paid mechanics remained in the courts or alleys. When the owner died, the property was put in control of an agent, with the usual result—rapid degeneracy. It was now conducted to secure the largest returns at the least outlay. The evils of the absentee landlord are not confined to Ireland. Absenteeism on the part of owners of tenement-house property is one of the causes of the social and civic problems that retard the growth of the highest civilization in New York. Under the management of an agent, the character of the tenants in the courts changed rapidly, and the people who took possession added to the disreputable character of the Fourth Ward. For years before this the largest per cent. of the immigrants settling in New York settled in this section. They came with distorted notions as to their place in the new land. Liberty meant to the majority the right to follow their own will. When hunger and loneliness and nakedness forced them to reconsider their first conception of what America was, resentment, recklessness, or adaptability developed. The difference was a matter of temperament quite as much as of race.

In 1880 the heads of the families living in the courts were day laborers—men who worked along the docks, coal shovelers, hucksters, women who did a day's work, sold newspapers at the ferries, or worked in the factories. Every child in the alley was ready to do anything that would earn money from the time he could walk. The people knew every benefit the city dispensed to the poor: free coal; homes available and how to get in them; free burial; every organization that dispersed charity, and how to get it. Even the children were clever in their extremities, and knew how to get assistance when the Island claimed their parents. From infancy the children looked forward to wage-earning as a time of happiness. School was a prison-house to be avoided, except when its warmth and shelter were preferable to the street, or the home, when intemperance and temper made life unendurable in it; then they attended school willingly. The truant officers in this region were not feared. They were the fags of the "boss," not the officers of a city department. None of the fads of to-day, which so disturb the conservative people who see ruin of mental ability in modern educational systems, were then thought of. The kindergarten, nature study, manual training, were on the educational horizon of New York, in a cloud scarcely so large as a man's hand. The trustee system was in perfect working order. The teachers were what God made them, unhampered by the pressure of superintendent and supervisors to maintain standards.

It was as true in that day as in 1892, when a man, wholly familiar with all the systems of education in the country, to the question, "Why is there such uniformity in the defects of the schools in the tenement-house regions?" replied, "They represent the demands of the people in the district who elect the men who control them. You will find that the public schools always represent the public sentiment and demands of the people interested in them."

This was profoundly true of the schools in this region at this time. To-day there is scarcely any change in the buildings except that of added age. At least two of them are a disgrace to the city. But there is a great change in the system. To-day the civilizing force in this community is the public schools; the remnant does not attract the philanthropist. To the men and women of our public schools who, preserving the highest ideals, work with enthusiasm amid the most discouraging surroundings, the city owes a debt that money cannot repay.

The liquor saloons numbered then about as they do now, occupying every available space. More elaborate now, perhaps, for they represent political headquarters, if not proprietorship, of men identified with the worst forms of political corruption; then, as now, openly used in the interest of these men. There is this great change, that children dare not now, as they did then, enter and leave these places fearlessly at any hour carrying pails, pitchers or bottles. It was then a neighborly kindness to let children thus serve a neighbor; it was a source of revenue to the children.

The gangs were many and notorious in the ward. Frequent were the clashes and loyal the spirit with which assailed and assailants maintained silence if there was danger of arrest because of these conflicts. "To squeal" was to earn the contempt of the community. The number of crimes, the full measure of degradation, reached in this ward will never be known. The dense population of this ward is so hidden by business and traffic that in 1901 the statement was made by some people interested in civic affairs that the region was given over to office buildings. The district of which the Fourth Ward is a part cast 10,000 votes in the mayoralty campaign of that year. Votes that represent a civilization as peculiarly its own as though oceans separated it from the people a mile and a half away.

Target companies were the social clubs of that

day, the forerunners of the political organizations of to-day. The climax of their existence were the annual excursions to some near-by grove for shooting matches. These matches were the great social occasions of the many "sets." The question of who was the reigning belle of the locality was settled beyond dispute by selection of one to present the wreath for the target, or a big bunch of flowers, to the captain of the target company on the day of the annual parade. These were always of artificial flowers, and were made gorgeous and splendid by floating strips and fringes of tinsel paper. The greatest feuds in the ward have grown out of the selection of the fair lady to present these trophies. Her selection changed the political history of her friends often, and her knights' fists fought her cause, and crowned her, their wounds testifying to their devotion. The political "boss" of that period presented the organizations that acknowledged his leadership with silver mugs, castors or pitchers—prizes for the shooters—but he presented money to keep the balance of his popularity. The gifts were carried conspicuously over the route of the procession, which always stopped in front of the house of the lady, who was to express her favor in the gifts of floral trophies—usually paid for by the company, sometimes by her knight, or knights combined for her honor. This house was for the time being the center of interest for the crowd, as she was of envy or pride to the community. The day of the target parade was one that called for great sacrifice, that it might be attended by the requisite formalities and new clothes. Money must be raised to provide barouches for the great political lights of the ward who gave this particular company their favor; to pay the attendant colored men who carried the target and the water and tin cups; for the band with the drum major. All cost money, and money was scarce; but the prominence and pleasure paid; and the Fourth Ward had many of these organizations, which made life exciting, and at times dangerous, when their several groups met, each struggling for supremacy, each with a leader who must be defended.

Fresh-air organizations, seaside resorts, were as unknown as trolleys; hundreds in the Fourth Ward lived and died without ever having seen Central Park or the ocean. The relief from the sufferings of summer was sitting and sleeping on the near-by piers. Man's humanity to man at this period of New York's social history was expressed in hospitals, infirmaries, homes of many kinds, distribution of food, clothes and medicine. The more applications secured for these sources of relief, the more tickets given out in a year at any point for outside relief, the more easy the conscience of the men who sent the money that maintained them, who measured the value of their charities by the figures representing human beings that appeared in the reports. Thanksgiving and Christmas dinners were then, as now, "roundups" for the wretched, the needy and the lazy. The pleasure of the givers was greatly added to by watching the hungry eating.

What caused the misery and wretchedness was no secret; but with few exceptions the men of money and brains were not ready to remove the prevailing and rooted cause. The exceptions were the men who, impressed by the example of Mr. Alfred T. White, leased the tenements known as Single and Double alley, or Gotham Court, the worst piece of property in what was acknowledged to be the worst ward in the city.

It had grown more and more difficult to collect rents, and the destruction of the property by the tenants made any effort at repair futile. Lead pipe, brass faucets, were wrenched off and sold as rapidly as they were put in; banisters, stair-rails, blinds, even wooden floors had been used as firewood. The very bricks on the chimneys were used as missiles of offense and defense. The Double Alley boasted of a haunted house, which at times created the greatest excitement in the neighborhood because of mysterious noises and lights seen and heard at night. Again and again the house had been raided by the police and stolen goods recovered after the ghostly exhibits. The police showed to the brave of the neighborhood that sulphur and brimstone were the ghostly lights, and clever arrangements of ropes and pulleys and pans the source of the cries and groans that had frozen them with fear. It was useless. The next appearance of the lights and the sound of awful groans filled the neighborhood with terror.

For obvious reasons the only source of water supply was a hydrant in the center of each alley. The only drainage was the sink sunk in front of it. When it is remembered that between five and six hundred people lived in these houses, the opportunities for cleanliness will be appreciated. All the water used was carried up and down stairs. That pans and pails of water were emptied from the windows without careful note of the passer-by beneath is not surprising. This naturally was not conducive to peace; but peace was not the aim of the people of the court; in fact, its disturbance varied the monotony of life in the alleys.

Single Alley had a narrow opening from its rear, or western, end to Roosevelt Street. This

THE SITE OF THE OLD RUNWAY.

was paved with brick sunken and broken. It was a dormitory for the drunken and homeless, a depository for all kinds of refuse. This alley was a runway. The entrance on the two streets offered every opportunity of escape to the fleeing fugitive from justice or vengeance. The code of honor of the alley was to speed the hunted and obstruct the hunter. The policeman entering the alley in pursuit of a transgressor knew his fate; he was a target for water, wood, coal, bricks and unlimited language; unexpected obstructions would be found in the alley, and the attentions he received when he tripped or fell were intended to increase the distance between the representative of law and order and the fleeing offender. He or she might or might not be a friend. The alley's activity in behalf of the fugitive was based on a new interpretation of the promised return of bread cast on the waters.

No matter how bitter the feuds that divided the tenants in the alley, the appearance of a rent collector in the later days healed the breach, bridged the widest chasm. He was a common foe and to be downed by common consent. If abuse and defiance did not drive him beyond the gates, bricks dropped from the roofs, after a vigorous campaign of water and cooking utensils, conducted by the feminine contingent from the windows, usually accomplished his complete rout, not only for that time, but for the future. As the years passed on, it became almost impossible to get any agent to make the second attempt to collect rent from the tenants of the alleys.

The home life of the people in the alley was interesting. Every inch of space was occupied. The families ranged from a childless old couple, past seventy, who had lived twenty-eight years in the Single Alley, to the boy and girl who had just started housekeeping on nothing at all. The women in the alleys had married, it was found, at about eighteen. They knew absolutely nothing of housekeeping. Many of them acknowledged that they had never made a fire before they married. The most elementary knowledge of cooking, sewing or the use of money was lacking. Of the two hundred and one mothers in the alley, one could cut and make the garments for herself and children; four could make bread—one did; one made soup sometimes, but could not remember the last time. Meals consisted of bread and coffee, or tea, with beer provided for "him" for breakfast and supper. Dinner was a "bit" of meat or fish, thought of and cooked between eleven and twelve; the cooking was frying. Potatoes were substituted for bread at this meal; rarely any other vegetable except Sunday. On that day, if there was money enough in the morning, dinner was of corned beef and cabbage, or bacon and cabbage. One family standing at the head of this community socially had meat three times each day. This family had in it five wage-earners. They paid four dollars a month rent for two rooms. The children had all been born and had grown to manhood and womanhood in the alley. As the writer was able to win the confidence of these people, it was evident that each mother was conscious that something was wrong that life yielded no better return. What was wrong? Where the remedy was to be found did not seem to interest them. The days drifted. Children ran half naked or in rags, while mothers sat in neighbors' rooms, stood in doorways, in the halls, or lounged in the alleys. There were homes in which neither needles, thread nor scissors could be found. The mother did not know how to use them. A pot and a frying pan were the only cooking utensils the most lavish closet revealed. Washing and scrubbing are laborious at any time, but when carrying water from ten to fifty feet on the level, then up one to four flights of stairs and down again is added to the labor, it is not astonishing that dishes, clothes and bodies were at all times freighted with disease and death. A knowledge of the relation between dirt and disease, cleanliness and health was not the general knowledge it is to-day. Their relation to moral elevation or degradation is barely understood to-day.

The average weekly wages of the men living in the alleys at this period was between eight and nine dollars per week, and sometimes kept at the latter figure for weeks. It will be seen at once that the poverty, misery, degradation and dirt that kept life at the level it was in the alleys was due to some other cause than wages, for rent was only four dollars a month, when paid, and it was paid less than eight months of the year. Beer flowed in the alley; tin cans, pitchers, pails, went back and forth at all times of the day and night. It was the first errand on which the baby feet were sent. Every woman in the alley acknowledged that she had seen her husband drunk before she married him. She knew better how to manage him when he was drunk than when he was sober. A blow given in drink was not recorded against a husband either by the wife or her neighbors. A blow given when the man was sober was remembered and aroused pity and sympathy. Over seventy per cent. of the women drank to the point of unconsciousness. All used liquor. Of child training there was none. The act that was laughed at this hour brought a blow the next. Attending school was for the child to decide. If he wanted to go, he went. Usually lack of clothing shut out about half the children of school age in the alley.

Mother love was largely a matter of animal instinct. While the baby depended on her for nourishment, she could be found with it in her arms at all times; it was, so far as life had a concentrated thought, her constant care. The moment the baby found its feet and used them, the child was cut loose and began his individual life. His standards, language, habits, were what his environment made them. His care, so far as the mother was concerned, was conducted on the lines of the least resistance. If the child was struck by an outsider, it raised the tiger in the mother; if ill, a burden to carry for which there was neither money nor knowledge; the mother had no strength and could not meet cares that demanded continuous thought; her mind was not trained to it. Health and disease were largely a matter of luck. Death brought pangs, but life was too much of a struggle for it to be a crushing blow, even when it was one's child. Children came and went too fast in the alleys for their coming or going to fill or empty even a mother's life.

Not one woman in the alley could remember ever having an entire new outfit in her life, nor had any of her children; her first baby had worn garments that had been made for some more fortunate baby.

Such was the dead level of existence lived in the alleys. Without the stimulus of drink it would be lethargy, and was when there was no money to treat or be treated. Pleasure? It was unknown outside of the beer can. If that did not give pleasure, why life was a hand-to-hand, hopeless struggle with homelessness, hunger and nakedness. In the alleys a fight became a pleasure and death a social opportunity. Even love seemed denied the people of the alleys. Marriage often was a part of the habitual drifting when not a matter of compulsion. Homes were established with no bond but that of law, and sometimes not that. That they even were what they were was a tribute to the fundamental morality that is the salvation of the civilized world.

These were the people who had made the alleys between 1855 and 1880, when the owners of the estate gladly leased the property on a long lease. As has been stated, spasmodic attempts had been made to reclaim the property, to make it productive, but always by men acting for the owners; they never came in personal contact with the tenants. It is doubtful if they even had any conception of the effect of their delegated responsibility on the people, or had any knowledge of the change that resulted when the property ceased to have the personal supervision of the owner.

The lessees put two ladies in control of the property. One or the other was to be found there each day.

The tenants were notified that rent must be paid weekly; that the rooms would be whitewashed and painted; that the agents would be at liberty to visit the rooms daily; that no child would be permitted to carry liquor on the premises; every bundle or basket carried by a child would be examined, and any liquor found would be emptied into the sink in the yard. Water would be put in the halls on each floor; destruction of property would mean eviction. All who were unwilling to accept these conditions were asked to move at once. The rent remained the same, four dollars per month for two rooms. Families desiring four rooms could have them for eight dollars per month, the company cutting a door through the party walls, giving direct ventilation through the floor, with windows opening on both alleys. The absolute impossibility of getting two equally good rooms in the neighborhood for the same rent kept the majority of the families. A few tacitly accepted the change, largely because acquiescence was their habit of mind, while some expected to set at naught any rules or regulations that they found obnoxious. No tenant moved voluntarily.

The new ownership took possession with the same human beings who had occupied the houses for years. The first step was to insist on cleanliness. The alleys were swept and washed every morning, as were the halls and stairways. Garbage cans were provided and their use insisted on. Every can or bundle carried by a child was examined, and all liquors found in them were emptied into the sink in the yard. Quarrels and fights grew less frequent, especially among the women. The children attended school, for their appearance during school hours led to investigations that the majority of the tenants preferred to avoid. The aim was to establish such relations between the representatives of the company and the tenants as would give opportunities to reduce the ignorance and indifference that were quite as responsible, if not more responsible, for the misery in the homes than lack of money. The tenants held aloof. They were tenants because they could not get as much comfort for the money elsewhere; but there could be no friendship where the payment of rent was insisted upon, where drunkenness involved the risk of, and abuse of property positive, eviction.

Several young couples were tenants. The aim and hope of the agents were to gain the confidence of these young mothers. The first child of one died late that summer. Potter's Field was the place of burial. The young father could have worked six days in the week, but that would have been slavery intolerable. He refused it, and followed his lifelong habit of drifting, which was also that of the young mother. She had never resented her husband's days of idleness until this baby died and there was not one cent to provide for the care and disposition of the little body. This was the opportunity of the two women who were waiting to prove that they were not oppressors. A little coffin, a white slip and socks, some flowers—at that time an unheard-of tribute to death—a carriage and a grave in the cemetery approved by the mother's church was provided. The battle was won. Every man, woman and child in the alley surrendered to this evidence of comradeship. That this act gave birth to hopes that must be stifled was natural. Rules must be enforced and comradeship expressed at the times of emergency. The first and hardest battle was won. Confidences were gained that led to marriages and baptisms that had been neglected or forgotten. The office, simply but tastefully furnished, became a schoolroom, where the mothers and the children learned to sew. Goods were bought in quantities and sold at cost to the learners. A sewing machine and a teacher appeared and were welcomed. Practical talks, or, more properly, conversations, were held; but no one took note of them as special efforts in philanthropy, they were so naturally a part of each day's experience. The daily visits to each tenant resulted in establishing relations that justified reproof, suggestion, commendation. The standards of pleasure, pain, suffering, accomplishment were elementary in the alleys. An hour's work with the needle left the worker exhausted, and diversion then meant moral safety. The homes were barren, and the acme of hope was wages to pay rent, buy food and clothes; the last rarely realized. The months, and even years, passed without the people passing beyond the confines of the ward. The generations lived this life, and it was a fixed habit. The world had nothing to offer to the habitual residents of the ward that the ward did not provide; it has but little to-day to offer them.

In spite of the emptiness of life and barrenness of these homes, they were on the whole better than the homes of the preceding generation.

When the wives laid the cause of their burdens on their husbands' shoulders because they drank. the question, "Did you know he drank when you married him?" would be answered easily, with no thought of self-condemnation, "Yes," in frank confession.

"Do you drink?"

"I drink beer, mostly. Sure, ye get discouraged just working and washing, and never a cent; not a decent rag to go on the street, and no place to go when you get there but a neighbor's house. What is there but a glass of beer? You don't mean to get drunk; yer that before ye know."

This total lack of personal relation to life was the mental attitude of almost every woman. If she was a widow, she worked to make a home for her children, who, again and again, so often that it ceased to attract attention, heard how much harder life was because they were in it. This seemed the accepted attitude, and accounted for the expression on the faces of these children—a puzzled, hardened expression that blotted out all suggestion of childhood. That time was an element in the problem of life was not accepted. That the garment made at home would last longer and cost less was conceded; but what was the use of making things when they could be bought so cheaply. The total absence of reasoning powers was shown here. To make soup would mean staying at home, thinking and planning for hours in advance of a meal. The soup would cost no more than steak and provide two meals, but it would mean loneliness, when the time, through ignorance, could not be turned to interesting uses.

There were women in these alleys, mothers of grown children, who could not tell a bias from a straight edge; who could not put a gingham apron together having straight and bias selvages. Beyond sewing on occasional buttons, there was no use in their minds for needles. They had worked in tin factories. They had worked at all kinds of employment that called into play the minimum amount of brains and the maximum of muscles. Not one woman was found who before her marriage had worked in any line of employment that had the slightest connection with the arts of home-making. The wages they earned was that of unskilled labor, in lines of employment known to be intermittent. Wages, large or small, went into the common family fund. The future was not a matter of care. When all in the family worked, life was lived merrily; when hard luck came, life was lived stoically. This spirit went into the home of the wage-earners when they married. There was far less physical suffering than the privations of their lives made natural. Often these limitations were self-imposed; there was money enough to give life color and purpose, if only there had been knowledge to guide in the adjustment between necessities and income; a conception of time as an element in the financial problem.

The closer one entered into the individual life,

YOUR CHOICE.

the more clearly was it revealed that the problems of poverty grew out of the inability to see the relations of things, to comprehend life in its entirety. Even after two years of close relation with these people in the alleys, it was with the utmost caution and tact that the subject of free coal could be broached. It was then distributed by the city—an intimate source of political corruption. A large quantity of coal was purchased and put in the cellar. It was offered to the tenants at the same price the grocer sold it by the pail, with the difference that it was delivered in the rooms. First, pride, a desire to appear somewhat above the neighbors, moved to independence on the coal question. In two years' time free coal was in the category of disgraces in the alley, and marked a rising moral tide.

A young woman and her husband were special objects of attention to the agents. They were young, good-looking, bright, and, when sober, ambitious as their conception of life made possible. Both drank, the woman more than the man, and she sank lower when drunk. For years she had spent more time on the Island than off it. What could be done? The whitewashing and painting of the two hopelessly barren rooms seemed to bring the woman to a pause. It was not possible to get beer through a neighbor's child now, and until she was drunk this woman would not go into a saloon. The clean alley, washed every morning, by some process of reasoning seemed to demand corresponding effort indoors, and the barren rooms were never dirty when the woman was sober. Even this gave employment to hands that had never used a needle, therefore less time was spent lounging in the doorway or other rooms. The washing of clothes, though ragged and few, took time and centered the interest, if but for a short time. The look of utter weariness and indifference in the face of the woman was slowly disappearing. There was really a purpose in life; the four walls and little else that was home required thought and effort. Life had an object at last. But the devil of drink was not so easily conquered; she was gone one morning from home. The neighbors explained to the agents her absence, being familiar with the habits of the type. In court she listened again indifferently to "Ten dollars or ten days." This time a woman came forward, paid the ten dollars, and Agnes was free. Surprised, dumb-stricken, wondering why, Agnes followed the friend home. New clothes, simple, suitable, were waiting for her. Then the fight began. At times it was hourly. Work was provided that the clumsy, untrained hands could do. The proceeds were to pay for a new carpet, that had to be unrolled many times to hold Agnes from the street. At last it was down, and the two friends added a rocker and a picture. Tom was a new man, and every penny of his wages came home. All this time the prosperity of the couple was viewed by most of the people as due to passing "good luck." That there was a moral battle being fought did not seem to enter their consciousness. Four years later, on the stairway, the writer saw Agnes with her beautiful baby boy, her first-born, on her arm. The comprehension of what the sight must have been on the Mount of Transfiguration has always been clearer when the expression on the face of Agnes, as she met the woman who had fought for her salvation for time and eternity, is recalled. Two years had passed since Agnes had tasted liquor in any form. Her passionate devotion to her baby, her new knowledge of the arts of home-making, kept her so busy that Agnes was rarely a visitor to her neighbors, except in the case of sickness. Tom's love of liquor seemed limited; largely a matter of companionship or discouragement. When his home became a center of interest to Agnes, his buoyant nature responded to the new environment. When liquor disappeared from the home, it ceased to be a constant temptation. Outside of his home Tom found for a time that his new departure attracted to him unpleasant attention, guying, teasing, coaxing, which he met with jokes. Force as an inducement to make him drink was met by blows; and Tom struck heavily. The new impulse for a better life brought heavy social penalties on Tom and Agnes. It meant nothing in common with those about them. When a man and woman will neither treat nor be treated at that social level social ostracism follows. Their home was the refuge of the children driven by frenzied, drunken parents from their own homes. What they had they shared with the children when the parents were on the Island. When sickness came to homes in the alleys, Tom and Agnes could be relied upon to share and help in carrying the added burdens. Tom's muscles and the knowledge of their power saved many a wife from blows that, without Tom, would have fallen freely. Back of their every effort stood the two wise women who were redeeming this corner of the great city. The day came when Tom and Agnes realized the boy must grow up in a different neighborhood, and Tom and Agnes moved.

The making of a laundry compelled the removal of a childless couple who had occupied their rooms over thirty years. It was impossible to make them accept the fact that the children could play in the alley under the new *régime*. For years the old woman and her stick were familiar to the sight and the feelings of the children of the alley. "I'm in Dixie's Land. Dixie ain't home!" had been shouted under their windows, at their room door, which was very near the alley door, to bring them out in torrents of rage. As age made the old couple less fleet and more quarrelsome, the daring of the children grew, and any time of the day or night the conflict between the old couple and the children, in which parents figured, was a possibility. Peace became impossible. The decision was final; the old couple must go; their rooms were necessary to the new improvements. It was pathetic to discover that no amount of persuasion would make the old couple live north of Roosevelt Street; it meant a lowering in their social world. "I've always lived respectable, and I always will. I would not live in that block," announced the old woman, with conscious pride. Even the alley, it was found, had standards of residence, a line that must not be crossed, to maintain respectability.

By this time the mental attitude of every woman in the alleys had changed toward her home. Positive determination to overcome inertia, or ambition to excel, it was impossible to create. Innate predilections were the chief factor in individual development among the women.

What a woman liked to do she attempted to learn how to do, or what she found she could do most easily. Some would learn to cook who absolutely refused to sew; some would sew who refused to cook; some would take care of the babies while the mothers were learning who would neither cook nor sew, feeling they could do both well enough; these it was impossible to make home-makers. The shackles of the past could never be thrown off wholly by the home-makers in the alleys. The children responded; could be won by personal affection, by prizes, by the mother's insistence. For it was soon learned that nimble fingers in the home lightened the mother's work; but the mothers were the unwilling victims of their own past.

The use of money was the most difficult lesson of all to teach. If there was money, the food was bought lavishly; pennies were given freely to the children. If there was no money, the barrenness was accepted even cheerfully. Wages were given at the maximum weekly amount remembered. No deductions were made for idle days. It requires a knowledge of advanced arithmetic to adjust intelligently forty weeks of wages to fifty-two weeks of expenses. It requires more than an elementary knowledge of arithmetic to adjust five days' wages to the seven days' expenses, fixed and emergency, of a growing family. When a week comes that brings six or seven days' wages, is it a marvel that in view of the many weeks of imposed restrictions this week of wealth should be welcomed as a period of freedom from care? That the money should be lavishly used? It takes the ability to think, to connect cause and effect, imagination, to see possible results, memory of experiences to hold men and women constantly in check, and this means mental training. Not a woman in the alley had attended school regularly during even the short period of her school life; each one had gone to work the moment she could earn money. Neither she nor any one about her questioned the value of the work she found to do beyond the money it gave at once. Nobody ever thought of the present as in relation to the future. Now that she was a mother, she met life the same way. Her children must earn money. To make sacrifices that their wage-earning capacity in the future might be greater would, if suggested to her, have been merely an evidence of how little the rich know of life. What was the estimate of life these mothers in the alley made? The differences between them were external, not mental. One answers for nearly all. To get as much comfort out of to-day as possible and to-morrow work hard, and be careful. To the majority that to be used to-morrow never came. When plenty came, it was always to-day—a glad, free day that might never come again.

At the end of four years but four of the tenants of the alleys who were tenants when the lease was executed had been evicted. The death rate had lowered from 85 to 22 per cent. The tenants rarely appeared in the police courts. Wife-beating created excitement and indignation. But in spite of the awakening, a moral, mental, physical inertia, stagnation, held more than the majority of the tenants in control. There was spasmodic response; but the painful truth had to be accepted that there must be redemptive power within to respond to redemptive conditions without before the home could be vitalized with the spirit of hope and energy. Fifty years and more of neglect and indifference cannot be overcome in five years of moral activity exerted to overcome the evils man neglected to prevent.

The alleys are gone; some tenants drifted to other scenes, more settled in the tall, dark tenements that have sprung up through the whole district, the worst type erected in New York. The rear buildings abound even back of the tall factories, reached by dark, noisome alleys. No amount of care or repair could save the old houses. They have gone the way of all material things. Their history is a part of the social and political history of New York.

How slowly moral sentiment grows in a large city is shown by the years that elapsed before active measures were taken to redeem what was known as a plague spot, a menace to the body politic, a constant source of moral degeneracy.

The Citizens' Association, organized in 1864, through its Council of Hygiene and Public Health, districted the city for special investigation by sanitary experts. One of these gives a large part of his report to Gotham Court, and presents sectional drawings to show the impossibility of securing proper sanitary conditions for the people living in the notorious houses. It seems incredible that these conditions once known should not have aroused public interest to the point of action. Nothing was done. The physical and moral degeneracy continued until 1880, when a few private individuals made the experiment of redemption. Even this came when the houses had gone beyond the point of reclaiming. On the site of the old buildings rises a new business building.

Not far away two of the most brutal and atrocious murders of recent years in New York have occurred. In July, 1901, three blocks from the old buildings, in broad daylight, a man known to be the collecting agent for property in the neighborhood was robbed by three members of a well-known gang. The children are thin, precocious. Their language, even in their play, is vulgar, coarse, profane. Babies have at their command strange oaths, probably never heard elsewhere. The streets are neglected, the sidewalks uneven and broken. For almost half a century this region has had a reputation peculiar to itself. Efforts have been made to reach the people, but they have not been persistent. Even the church efforts are perfunctory, as though faith as to the redemptive power in this people did not exist.

This fact remains: within the boundaries of this region lives a community that is shaping the political control of New York City and State, and will for years to come. It has its traditions of loyalty; it has fixed standards of its own peculiar privileges; its standards of rights. The very police of the region expect certain things to occur; misdemeanors of a certain character that would bring punishment anywhere else are passed by here; they are part of the civilization of the region. Snuggled down under the shadow of the bridge and the elevated road, a center of business interests which the moral standards of the residents do not affect, because their activities, other than of the muscles, are not exercised until carts, drays, drivers, clerks, proprietors have gone northward or across the river. The community lives within itself, has created its own standards, and is New York in its own estimation.

Writing of the people in this section in 1865, a sanitary expert quotes with an apology a medical term common in the hospitals and dispensaries as a disease of the people in this section, "tenement-house rot." The term has, perhaps, in the interests of civilization, died out; but no one can walk through these streets, observing the faces of the people, and not realize that the old, unsanitary, germ-laden tenements of this section have produced a physical condition peculiar to this region, as it has a moral degeneracy that is peculiarly its own. The section, as a whole, has not attracted the philanthropist. He is wise in his day and generation and puts forth his efforts where the tide of humanity is rising, and not falling, even though it means three or four generations before the tide is out.

New York has a gospel all its own. Work where the crowds are greatest, that the printed reports may count people in great numbers, for ye gain dollars thereby. New York counts the remnant only at the polls, and ignores the penalty her indifference imposes on her own advancement.

The opening years of the century hold promise that there is at least a partial realization of the solidarity of the interest of the people. That conditions make for degradation in the homes means degradation of citizens; and this means burdens laid, not on the sections where the homes and the citizens are found, but on the whole city. What altruism has not accomplished, selfishness may. It may be that where all else has failed, intelligent politics may redeem, and the section again may be the center of the moral as well as commercial activity.

CHAPTER II.

THE DEVELOPMENT OF SOCIAL CENTERS.

THE centralization of the interests of the tenement-house population is not understood by those who broaden their mental, if not their active, interest by reading and travel; who in the varied interest of a broader life are forced to see the multiplicity of factors that enter into the settlement of every problem. This is what we mean by knowing the relation of things; marking the distinction between those who see only and those who comprehend. The man who is a machine set in the place where he bears his relation to the whole by an authority which he dares not question loses all opportunity to comprehend his relation to that whole. He is interested in immediate results as related to himself only. This is the relation which the mass of the tenement-house workers and voters bear to life.

The people of whole sections live entirely within certain geographical lines, every interest centered within these limits.

The race sections are logical, based on the law

of natural selection; of family interest. The first generation of immigrants naturally hold the second generation of home-makers near them, and these together hold the relatives and friends who follow. Three generations are not infrequently found in the same house, each maintaining its own home. The new arrivals keep alive the foreign home traditions, the foreign home habits of living. Poverty and greed make the people crowd together. The last arrivals are taught what their predecessors have learned of American life and law. The race section perpetuates itself; it retains all that it can of the old life, and interprets the new according to the lessons learned from environment, and power as it is exercised on the people. Each race section has its own thoroughfare. The people on the street use their own language, and trade in shops of their own countrymen. In some sections newspapers are published in the language of the section, giving prominence to the local news. Were it not for the public schools, one wonders what would be the result of this race centralization.

The writer once met a man who had voted for twenty-three years in one ward. For sixteen of these years he had cast his vote from one house in Orchard Street. He had never been farther north than Houston Street, farther south than Hes-

SATURDAY MORNING ON THE EAST SIDE.

ter and had never crossed the Bowery. He had positive convictions on every subject relating to the ward; he knew the life history of every political leader in that portion of the city; could rehearse the disasters that had followed every man who failed to fall in line at the polls; knew what saloon-keepers were forced to obey the law, and who "didn't care a cent" for the law; knew why this man could put his goods on the walk and why the other man could not. He protected his own two daughters from the evils of his home environment as he saw them; was strict to rigorousness about their home-coming; watched the kind of people who moved into the house in which he lived, and doubtless kept it above the average of the neighborhood by his watchfulness. But he did not know who was President of the United States, and did not consider it the business of the poor man. He refused a "job" under the city, because he didn't want to be "beholden." It was all right for the man who needed a job to take it. The only grievance the man had was that the Hebrews were crowding into the neighborhood. This was an invasion of his personal rights; they had their own place on the south side of Grand Street, as the Italians had west of the Bowery, and coming into that region north of Grand Street was an intrusion on the personal rights of himself and his countrymen. The first thing which would happen, if they—his own people—did not look sharp, would be the Hebrews would have a say in politics. The man's mental attitude is typical of the race settlement, the race political rights theory in many sections of New York; the difference is only in the race dominant.

This man was a porter, who for seventeen years was employed in an East Side department store, working in a sub-cellar nine hours a day for nine dollars a week. He could not read, though he came to this country when five years of age. He became a wage-earner at eleven. His daughters became wage-earners at fourteen, having attended public schools until that age. The pride with which this man referred to his daughters' education made one comprehend the gradual absorption by the foreign peoples who come to us of American ideas. Those girls knew they were not educated; they had been forced to contrast their mental equipment with that of the "club ladies," as they called the residents at the College Settlement, where the club of which they were members met. They, too, had been satisfied until brought into relationship with those who represented another world. The revelation, because of contact with the minds of these college-trained women, showed them, so far as they could comprehend it, their own lack of mental training, the first step in their true education.

Women are by nature more conservative than men; they cling longer to early traditions and habits; find it more difficult to adopt new habits of thought. The more closely they are surrounded by people of their own way of life, their own habits of thinking, the more strongly intrenched are they in the customs and habits of their native country, the less are the homes they regulate modified by the new environment. The result is that whole sections of New York to-day arc as foreign as the villages from which the people in them came. There are women in New York whose children and grandchildren were born in the city who cannot speak English, nor understand it beyond the merest assent or dissent. Their lives in old age are pitiable.

A sweet, motherly German once said to the writer, and but a short time ago: "I am so lonely. I cannot speak English. I never learn it. I sit in my daughter's house, where German is not used. The children all want to be Americans; they will not talk German. When I sit at the table, I never speak. They all talk, but I do not understand. Sometimes I ask, and the children say they have not time to tell me. They buy only the English papers, and so I cannot read. I wish

I had learned English when I first came. I was young then, but I had eight children after I came here, and I did everything for them. I could not take the time, I thought. I see now the children could have taught me. Now they have not the time." This woman was a German in her sympathies, her interests, her standards. Positive race antagonism existed between her and her family. She measured everything by German life and rule, and lived a critic among a people her own only in blood. In answer to the question, she explained that her husband learned English for his "work." The family attended the mission church when they attended church. She attended the German services, but the rest of the family, even her husband, the English services. Her constant plaint was: "I am so lonely. Some day I never speak all day. At the table they speak English."

Hundreds of women like this one sit in homes in New York in which they have no part, barred out by the fact that they speak a foreign tongue. One of the mistakes made in even our church work has been the maintaining of distinctive church services in a foreign tongue. In so far as the churches have done this, they have been an obstruction to good citizenship for time, whatever they may have accomplished for eternity, for the people they call their own.

One of the most earnest of missionary workers in New York, an American citizen born in Italy, protested vigorously to the writer on the policy of maintaining church services in New York in a foreign tongue. "You cannot make a united people using many languages. I would preach that to the people all the time. I use English words in my sermons to my own people, and I tell them to learn English; it is better for them in business. The women ought to learn, for they lose their children. They go away from them because they do not speak the English. In New York they are the victims of oppression, my people, because they cannot speak English. They have to bow the head to the yoke because they are foreigners in a strange land in which they vote. It is a great wrong to them and to the country. It makes the 'boss.' "

The first interest of the mother in the tenement, as of the mother everywhere, is the support of her children; to get for them all that she can. She would prefer that her husband should be honest, which may mean that the only dishonesty of which she has any comprehension is stealing money or other tangible property. In politics the tenement-house women have only a secondary interest. They accept without question the statements of their male relatives as to issues and men.

Even this degree of interest represents only the most intelligent of the tenement-house women. The charge that a man used his political position and affiliations to further his own advancement, that he purchased the votes and enthusiasms of less clever voters, would mean to the women educated in their conception of right and wrong under the systems of machine politics that the man was intelligent and trying to do the best he could for his family and his friends. To say that he refused to rally voters to support the party that gave him a position because he was convinced that the party was dishonest in the use it made of the victory it gained at the polls, would arouse the deepest contempt for the man. He would be considered not only untrue to his family, but to his friends. Had he remained in close relation to the politicians who gave him his chance, he would not only provide for his family, but his friends would have the benefit of his influence; he could give them a chance in time.

The man of brains they see drop his tools, take off his overalls and stand in high hat, and eventually frock-coat, the center of a crowd of men who smile at his nod, though they worked shoulder to shoulder but a short time ago—in a trench, perhaps; yes, even came over in the same ship with

THE PAST, PRESENT AND MIDDLE PERIOD.

him. The women do not understand the process of evolution, but they see the results. They soon know that from street sweeper to car conductor, the man who has become a politician under a strong partisan government regulates, and often decides, the wage-earning opportunities of the greater portion of the men in the tenement-house sections. They learn, these women, that it is not a question of how faithful the worker is in the discharge of his duty that insures him work, but that it is some mysterious influence they call "politics," that means work and wages or no work and no wages, and suffering. This conception of the relation of the petty politician to the voters' chance to earn even a meager and uncertain living under the sway of his influence rarely excites more than passing indignation from the women who suffer most because of the system. When the women of the politician's family grow arrogant and snobbish, then the floods of eloquence break loose for a time, and the listener may learn many things of which he would otherwise be ignorant. The increased power of the petty henchman rarely enables him to change the way of living of his family. Sometimes he does not when he can, for he knows that he increases his power as he lives on the level of the average voter in his district. The less conscience he has, the more patient he is in waiting for the day when his district is only one factor in his political strength.

Even the little children reveal deference to the family of the man who is known to have "pull." There came to an East Side library one afternoon a little girl better dressed than any child who had yet appeared there. She was impudent, noisy, aggressive. In the game-room she cheated in the games, and finally broke up several games of checkers and dominoes by pushing over the boards. No child resented this. The little girl when spoken to seemed astonished by the reprimand. As she was leaving, the writer said to her: "I am sorry, little girl, but I shall have to tell you that you must not come here again unless you mean to obey; you must not talk in the reading-room, and in the games you must play fair. I hope I shall not have to tell you not to come here again." The child stared in astonishment. She went out on the street. In a few minutes several little girls who had frequented the rooms for months came running back in great excitement, one saying breathlessly: "Why, that little girl's father is a school trustee; she does just as she likes in school." "Yes," added another, "and now she says she won't come here any more. She's awful mad." From her point of view this was a calamity. "Well, I hope she will not come if she cannot behave," was the comment made. The children stood aghast. The trustee system had been abolished in New York at least two years when this incident occurred. Later the writer found that the father was in the council of Tammany Hall.

A boy of the same neighborhood rang the bell, interfered with children leaving the house, and broke the windows. The time for kindly persuasion ended. When the members of a woman's club in that section using that house were consulted, it was made perfectly clear to the writer that worse troubles would follow if the boy were arrested, for he would not be detained and he would be more ugly than ever. His father was a ward leader who had formerly been a street sweeper, then foreman of the gang, etc., going through the gradations that mark the making of the minor "boss." This boy bullied little children, stole their toys, would break up their games. Yet to have him join in their play was evidently an honor which they bore much to retain. He was only fourteen, yet he was found to be the leader of a gang of boys in the most disgusting immoralities. Even this did not rouse the mothers of the neighborhood to fight for their children's protection. The boy was spreading immorality of a disgusting nature through a whole neighborhood. The evil he wrought was told in tears in private, but denied in public through fear of the father's power in preventing the accusers' husbands and sons from getting work—one result of the Tammany system that enslaves homes and blasts the innocence of little children in New York.

A clever, hard-working Irish woman was once telling the writer the story of her life and that of her children. At the time she was deeply interested in the future of four nephews, who were the motherless sons of her brother. Out of her experience with sons-in-law she enunciated her conclusions: "I tell me brother, don't let them b'ys learn politics; it's a mighty poor thrade. Sure, when Tammany's in they're all right; but when Tammany's out, where are they? Sure, it's a mighty poor thrade, as I learnt to me sorrer. Betther have them blacksmiths, sez I, like their grandfather at home. I do hope he be's listening to me, for they're foine b'ys." It will be easier for the four "b'ys" to learn politics than any other "thrade," for it is an open union making one demand, obedience to the "boss."

To this woman Tammany was an employer good to the poor man—a doctrine that is taught to the smallest boy. He breathes it in the air; he nurses it in the milk that nourishes him. As he gets older he adds a new article to his faith. The Tammany system is the protector of his liberties. It does not restrict him in his right of private judgment. As one studies the race sections, the discovery is made that hundreds of votes are cast for Tammany candidates in the belief that obnoxious restrictions on the sale of liquor on Sundays will be removed, or that the laws will not be enforced. The hope of raising the moral tone of the voters is futile while any portion of them justify the casting of a ballot for the sole reason that it will make it possible for the voter to break the law with impunity. The most demoralizing legislation is that which makes a man a sneak as well as a law-breaker. May the day be hastened when no man who stands in moral rectitude in the presence of man and God will be forced to maintain what he believes his rights in defiance of the law. We are a cosmopolitan country, owing power and greatness to the sons and daughters of many lands. The Puritan conception of government is out of place to-day. The larger conception of man not controlled by the law, but the master in himself of the restraints it would place upon him, is the American conception of manhood, and toward this the best legislative action must trend. Thinking men and women who have studied the social conditions of New York know that no more calamitous influence is set in motion in New York than a sense of injustice that protects and justifies to the people the breaking of a law. When this goes farther, and any considerable number of the citizens combine for the purpose of overcoming it by defying or by ignoring it, the foundations of the government are threatened. It is time for fanaticism to feel the pressure of broad-minded balanced public opinion. A law administered at the demand and according to the conscience of people unaffected by its administration, used by them against an equally intelligent class who feel that personal liberty has been curtailed at the expense of their right of judgment, is class legislation. No greater evil influence has been active in New York than the creating of a sentiment that endorsed the breaking of the liquor laws. It has been a prolific source of blackmail; it has enabled politicians, who live at the public expense, to pose to men whose personal right of judgment had been curtailed as the apostles of freedom. The short-sighted friends of temperance have by their misdirected activities created political capital for the men who in official life have made New York's problems.

Legislation enacted without the will of the people governed is provocative of two things: contempt and defiance of the law; unrest that makes for antagonism to government. The lower in the scale of reason the voter is, the less able he is to get any point of view but his own. His comprehension of the rights of others depends on the comprehension of his rights expressed in the law designed for his regeneration. He certainly never goes higher in the scale of reason while he defies the law in satisfying his sense of justice and freedom; he cannot rise in the scale of living while he stoops to acts he would avoid if his sense of justice were not outraged. He justifies his act because of his sense of oppression. He cannot respond to any effort looking to the general good of the city while he smarts under a sense of liberties curtailed by the very people who ask for his help.

When President Roosevelt was Police Commissioner he enforced the law governing the sale of liquor on Sunday. The city was torn asunder for weeks. The discussion filled the columns of the daily press. The fact, after weeks of discussion with one group of tenement-house women—all the wives of skilled workers—was finally made clear that the law was at fault, if fault there was, not the Commissioner. The law, if bad, must be repealed; but as long as it was the law it must be enforced. During this discussion much light was obtained. One woman told how cleverly the law was evaded by the liquor dealer two doors from her house. He hired the back room on the top floor of the house next door, keeping the liquor in a closet. The men in the secret entered the house two doors distant, went up to the roof and down the scuttle to the room where the liquor was to be had. Some of the group listened to her description with flashing eyes. When she finished she was given to understand that she had played the part of traitor. It was all right for her to do it. She was safe. Her husband was in a good, independent position; it made no difference to him how much trouble came because of her "telling tales." To others it was a disgrace that men who had only a few cents to spend for a little pleasure with their friends should have to sneak like thieves, as one of the women expressed it. All condemned having the liquor in their own homes in quantities, as they condemned the illegal selling. "When a man sneaks in like that he stays longer and spends more than when he can walk in openly and walk out again as he does other days. When he has it in the house he never stops treating and drinking until it's gone." The "free lunch" was deplored; but every one of the forty-five women decided that it was the only meal fit to eat that hundreds of laboring men ever had; that men were forced to eat at lunch counters in barrooms and buy liquor who would never go there if their mothers and wives knew how to cook. They claimed that the women would cook for their families if they knew how. They did not know how. They were forced to go to work in factories as soon as they left school, and never had a chance to learn anything about housekeeping; their mothers never knew how to keep house. Could a stronger argument for domestic science teaching in our public schools be advanced?

When the High License bill was before the Legislature at Albany several years ago, the writer was asked to speak at a mothers' meeting in one of the poorest sections of what was then the city of Brooklyn. On her way to the mission she counted nineteen liquor saloons on three blocks; in every case they were on the lower floor of a tenement house. The hall was over a pork and provision store; a loft without any attempt at more than broom cleanliness, walls bare, grimy, and seeming to ooze grease. The atmosphere of smoked meat was sickening. Nothing in the way of a shelter could have been more barren and repellent, yet it was a mission maintained by a church.

About one hundred women—the wives of day laborers and longshoremen—were present. Some were bareheaded; several with babies in their arms. The subject chosen was the High License bill. It was a discussion. At least ten of the women spoke. The scene will never be forgotten. One woman, about thirty, after listening intently, rose with a baby on her arm, and turning passionately to those in the hall, said: "Why don't yer talk honest? Every one of us drink. Some of us, not many, drink because we love it. Most of us drink because we're discouraged and don't know what else to do. We're fools; it don't help us; it makes it worse. Some of us would never touch it if it were not brought to us. We know that anything that would take away the drink from our doors would save us. Drive them out!" She turned to the platform appealingly. "Drive them out, so that we, yes, and the men, would have to walk four or five blocks to them, and we'll be different. It is easy sending the children now. Make it harder! Make it harder!"

"Shall we close them?"

"You couldn't do it," she said. "You couldn't do that. Make it cost more to start them, and there won't be so many. They'll be farther apart, and they won't try so hard to make us drink. Many a woman has learned to drink because she had to pass the holes to get to her home. Tell the truth like me, or say whether I'm telling the truth!" was her appeal to the audience.

The flood-gates were opened. Every woman agreed with the first speaker that the saloon could never be abolished; it could be regulated. Beer, they thought, to most women was a greater temptation than strong liquors. The number of saloons near their homes they thought the heaviest burden the poor man's family had to bear. They understood perfectly that the brewers paid for the licenses, and that the saloons were the meeting places where votes were controlled. They thought the saloons ought to be open at least Sunday afternoon, but they would have them close earlier Saturday night. They thought that any law that made a man a sneak to get a drink was an evil. They saw that such a law enabled the politician to say which man could sell liquor and which could not. One of them, who could neither read nor write, had discovered that the saloons selling a certain brewer's beer had more freedom than any of the saloons selling other beers; they thought the saloon-keepers paid either in money or drinks for the votes of the men who frequented their places in the interest of the politicians who owned the saloons or protected them. There was not the slightest evidence that one woman there saw any dishonesty in the system. There were no principles in politics, only men. Things remained with them the same no matter who was elected. It was a district which was under the control of one party, having an unquestioned majority, which steadily increased through the efforts of a shrewd leader who had no visible means of support.

The section in which this group of women lived was a long, narrow strip bordering on the East River. The residences of a population each occupying its own house at this time held the reeking tenements in check on the east. Within ten years this has been wholly changed. The handsome old residences have become tenement houses, overcrowded, uncared for, occupied by people now at the level of former despised neighbors. The better class of the laborers' families have left the houses bordering on the river, and these have been given over to the poorest and most hopeless of the day laborers. There is a thoroughfare which has stores brilliantly lighted for five blocks. Every want of the people can be supplied in them. The people, old and young, settle placidly in the region. It is their world. The language of the little children on the streets, from early morning until late at night, is appalling. A kindergarten was started,

A SOCIAL CENTER BECOMES POLITICAL.

but the people who started it did not have money enough to secure the right kind of a room, nor to make the room attractive, nor to keep it so clean that that would in itself make it more attractive than the homes of the children. It was finally given up, because even the small amount expended was not forthcoming at the end of the third year. It could have had four times the number of children the room would accommodate at one time, but no one cared enough to support it.

The half-grown boys are coarse-looking, use profane and coarse language unknowingly in their ordinary conversation on the street. Their attitude toward girls is brutal. The girls of this section are free in their manners, slangy and coarse in their conversation. They earn the lowest wages paid to women in the factories and lofts that abound in the region. The schoolhouses are old and dark; the streets are neglected and dirty. The smoky, grimy mission-room disappeared long ago. Not one influence is at work to raise the general moral tone of this community, the voting power of which outnumbers four to one regions where every influence in and out of the homes tends to develop moral standards and political intelligence in the same political unit.

The region is a social plague spot, neglected and allowed to spread. It does not present as a special feature to arouse activity the evils of the "Red Light" district, but only the blasting influence of a region sunk in the apathy of deadened moral natures, killed by the hopelessness of changing the environment of their homes until it represents all they ask of life. The poverty of the people makes well-nourished bodies impossible, and lack of physical power makes moral resistance impossible.

Recently in one of the most crowded of the tenement-house sections of New York, where the grip of poverty holds degradation, where the people live as remote from American civilization as when in their own land, the writer viewed the parade in the evening of the voters of the district, who had been the guests of the district leader, a State Senator, at an outing. These outings are the annual "round-ups" of the voters. The expenses of these outings run into the five figures, it is said, in this district. Boats and a grove are hired. Chowder, coffee, sandwiches and beer are provided free. Games of chance, to which, it is whispered, the district leaders are not disinterested observers, and athletics are the features of the outings. The return at night is an occasion for fireworks and a parade. Caps and canes are provided for the voters often; sometimes only a ribbon badge. The expenses are met by the sale of tickets, which sometimes sell as high as five dollars. These tickets the liquor dealers, in fact, the tradesmen of all kinds in the district, men holding office under the city government who are affiliated with the leader and the men who hope to secure rights or privileges, legal or illegal, through the leader's influence, know it is wise to purchase. To the mass of the men of the district it means perhaps the one day of freedom in the year, when they have the pleasure of enjoying drinks and food wholly at the cost of another.

In this particular parade were five thousand men, not one thousand of whom bore the slightest outward evidence of American citizenship, but the right to vote, as their presence in the column indicated. It scarcely seemed possible that the scene was in America. Swarthy women and children crowded gayly decorated fire-escapes, crowded the windows, and made movement impossible on the streets. Arches of lights, lanterns swinging from fire-escapes and on ropes from sidewalks to roofs, were in the colors of the land from which these people came. The flags and bunting displayed presented colors of a foreign land, with here and there the flag of the country whose political destiny their votes controlled to a large degree. The next day the white caps worn by the men in this parade appeared on the heads of schoolboys and working boys by the hundred, the wearers proud to wear the colors of the man who, so far as their knowledge or experience, or that of their parents, went, was the greatest man, the man of the widest range of authority, in the United States. What do they care who is at the head of the city government? The men do not need to ask who is the district leader; he finds them through his unpaid workers and the coalition is accomplished. Soon the immigrant, turned citizen, understands the principle. He gets work and votes for the leader. It is simple and direct. When the extent of one's knowledge enables him to handle a broom or to sell peanuts or bananas in the new country, and that under the supervision of a blue-coated tyrant who levies on the voter's cart, if not his pocket, when and where he pleases, moral arguments in a foreign tongue are not convincing to that voter. He would rather not submit to the supervision and its attendant tax; he would rather not have his work intermittent; but he learns that protest increases his evils, and he submits. The blue-coated tyrant is a friend of the "boss" who helped get his license, and it must be right. Whatever comes to him, he must not antagonize the "boss." That is the first lesson he learns in American citizenship, at the point where it is most effective, his wage-earning privileges.

A DOORWAY ON THE EAST SIDE.

There are leaders so strong and tactful that year after year their reign is unquestioned. Only the police and the ambulance surgeons know when there is an attempted revolution—when the leader's right is questioned by another would-be leader. There is only one issue—the man; nobody cares for the principle—if there be a difference of principle—involved.

In one of the old sections of the city in which is a ward that for forty years has excelled in crime; a section which at the present time presents the meanest and lowest of the tenements in New York; in which there is less effort to counteract the evils of the environment of the homes or change the environment due to the control of the "boss" than in any other section, a political feud culminated in the fall of 1901, defeating the man who had been the leader for years. It was stated that the man who won had expended $35,000; the man who lost, $12,000 in the struggle. This is a section where poverty is the universal inheritance of the people who make this section home.

For weeks the section was in a condition of constant warfare. The smallest boys were organized as gangs and shouted the name of the leader they had chosen their hero. Boys of five wore the buttons of their heroes. From fire-escapes, on wagons hung bits of white cloth declaring the names of the contestants. One of these, to avoid unpleasant embarrassment, had gone to California after the Lexow investigation. A favorite legend displayed by his enemy's friends was, "Paddy is the man who to Californy ran." This was displayed on one fire-escape on which opened the windows of two families, each espousing the cause of the contending leaders. The week before the balloting for leader the legend was kept in place by the constant vigilance for twenty-four hours of the day by the family whose sentiments it expressed. "Paddy" was defeated. The next morning the two neighbors, who had been enemies for weeks, leaned, each from her own window, chatting amicably, while the son of one was arranging the legend on the fire-escape to include both families. On either side was gracefully arranged an American flag, while the harp of Erin hung just in the middle of the fire-escape. Peace reigned in Warsaw. "Paddy's" friends, like the fairies of childhood, disappeared in the night. The whole district, as one man, accepted the change of rulers, and the new leader's banners were thrown to the breeze everywhere. Nothing succeeds like success in the tenement-house regions. For a couple of weeks peace seemed to reign in the district. The followers of the old leader found themselves displaced; new followers controlled the favors in the district. There began a new distribution of patronage. Then the old leader's displaced friends, with a few loyal souls, rallied about him. He had made money enough through his political affiliations to be defiant, and announced that the political corruption of the party to which he had belonged compelled him to rally to the support of the movement to overthrow it. Some of his followers were loyal to bravery, and declared, too, against the political system. Two of them, because of these declarations, were discharged forty-eight hours later from places in a city department where they drew salaries of $1200 per year. Their places were given to two of the new leader's followers. Two weeks later all had returned to the old allegiance, and the papers announced that the head of the Tammany system had decided that the patronage of the district would be evenly divided between the two factions.

Independence of action is costly under such a system; costly in loss of wages to the voter; of food, raiment, shelter to his family.

A voter who refuses to surrender the ease of his home or the pleasure of his club for the good of the district in which his home is located is not in a position to criticise his poor neighbor who will not jeopardize the position secured by his vote that supports his family to maintain the theory of American citizenship. Why should he make sacrifices to free the city from disgrace when his independent neighbor refuses to sacrifice his ease to protect his family from the inevitable evils of a corrupt city government?

It was the conferring the rights of citizenship on immigrants almost as soon as they landed that fastened on New York an evil that has grown until the city has been held in the shackles of a spoils system that overshadows its commercial supremacy and makes it the argument against democratic government. The heaviest disgrace for this condition rests not on the men who profit by the system but on the good men who permit it to develop. It was the logical result of their indifference to the city's good and their responsibility for that good. This inactivity on the part of the mass of responsible citizens made the control of the city offices for personal ends easy to the men who, because of lack of training and moral turpitude, could not conceive of a service for other than personal ends. Shrewdness made them see that the immigrant was the ladder on which they could climb to political power and stability. They met the immigrant as friend and neighbor; they secured him work; they schooled him to citizenship, and

EARLY MORNING AMONG THE PUSHCARTS.

began at once to train him in that deadliest of all influences in a democracy, class in politics. So long as this system of education prevails, the appearance of a candidate for local office who does not bear the "hall-mark" of the neighborhood will be resented.

As time went on and the immigrants came from many countries, a new evil sprang up—the race section; the section where, maintaining all the characteristics of the country from which the people came, the men exercise the rights of citizenship at the behest of a political trainer who is able to promise favors for obedience, and work vengeance for disobedience. Behind him is a power which he must obey until the day comes when by his own shrewdness he is able to cross swords with those above him in the political system, becoming himself a dictator. In the process of his evolution from ward heeler to district leader he has trained those who follow him so well that he duplicates himself scores of times, increasing his power every time he makes a follower, either by fear or favor, perpetuating the system that makes the city, as has been aptly said, a "gold mine" which it costs the operators nothing to work.

The man at the bottom knows the duplicate of the leader nearest his own level; this man is his friend, his countryman often. The links in the chain are unbroken, and the man who dares to disobey the orders issued from the top feels not only the displeasure of the henchman, but the combined strength of the chain, or as much of it as is necessary to compel him to obey or to crush him. The poor man whose tool to earn a living is a shovel, a pick or a broom is not in a position to defend his rights; he has no public sentiment in the only world he knows to support him in any attempt he may make to attain his rights when defrauded by the political system he, in utter ignorance, has helped to establish. When he is thrown out of work given to secure his vote, he has no redress. The man at the bottom must make the rule of his life "Small favors thankfully received." His hope for work in the future depends on keeping in friendly touch with the system; this is the first principle of American citizenship grasped by the naturalized citizen.

Just before our last national election a number of men employed in skilled labor in one of our city departments were laid off. To some of those men this loss of work meant suffering for their families; to others it meant debt and dependence. It was startling the spirit in which this loss of work and wages were accepted by these men. The district leader, elected by the people to make the laws at Albany, in order "to hold his district in line" for this election, had to provide forty-eight voters with places. He demanded from the department forty-eight places; the work was in his district. No one questioned his right to make this demand; these places represented his political capital. In no way could his demands be met except by the discharge of forty-eight men then at work who lived outside the district. It was done. The men laid off, almost to a man, accepted it as the fortune of the political protégé. Scarcely a word of resentment was expressed. There were removals into this special district before the next municipal election, and new enrollments under the leader's banner, irrespective of the political bias of the voters. Some of the men were sullen and felt the loss of manhood; some said, "I'll vote as I like, but I must have work;" others believed that only under this leader's banner could a poor man hope to get his rights—the privilege to earn his living; or, in their language, "He is hustling for his friends."

Not only does the skilled and unskilled manual laborer find that the approval of his district leaders is necessary to secure work under the city, but that the affiliations and power of the district leader and his political followers can secure him work under corporations holding public franchises. He knows that the district leader secures privileges, licenses, votes for franchises, directly or indirectly, with the distinct understanding that his recommendations insure places to the men who carry them. Under corrupt city government the man in business who does not cater to the political powers finds his privileges curtailed; that he is made the target for petty annoyances. Especially is this true in the downtown districts, where in the transaction of business the rights of citizens to the streets are ignored. Until one has lived close to it, it is almost impossible to believe the power over the working masses the smallest cog in the political machine exercises. It is this that makes imperative the control of the city by men of high moral standing. No amount of unselfish philanthropy can save a city governed by the corrupt.

There are sections in the city of New York where from the time the boy is old enough to recognize the power of a policeman he guides his life to curry favor with this visible expression of power. He knows almost as soon as he can talk the man who rules in the world in which he lives. He sees his playmate defy the policeman because his father is a man of power, or the friend of the man who rules the district. "Pull" is the law, all the law he recognizes. He hears discussed from his earliest years the dependence of his class on the political powers who govern, not for the good of the city, but that they may have their rights; their rights, as interpreted, being the securing of a place for a longer or shorter period at the nod of a "boss." Their district is all the city thousands of the inhabitants of these sections know. How can it be otherwise? They are never called for any purpose to any other part of the city, unless it be the cemetery. Family, friends, business all center within a score of blocks. If a distance must be traversed, it is through thoroughfares that but duplicate regions they know, all a part of the kingdom of the "boss."

When the observer sees five thousand men walking behind a banner conferred on the leader of the district because every man in it who votes votes at his dictation, there comes to him a faint apprehension of what political power in the tenement-house district is. This district leader interprets all these men know of this country or its institutions. They know that he secures work for them; that he befriends them in time of trouble. He interprets Christ's doctrine to them: "I was hungry and ye gave me meat; thirsty and ye gave me drink. I was a stranger and ye took me in; naked and ye clothed me; I was sick and ye visited me; I was in prison and ye came unto me." This is what the district leader does, if not in person, by proxy. Is it any wonder he can control votes? Is it any wonder that the poor, ignorant, unequipped voter should curry favor, bow to him, acknowledge his supremacy even to the law? For this the voter can break the law, and the leader secure remission of the penalty. The leader's nod has been known to guide the judge on the bench. The leader can make the innocent suffer because his power is greater than the law to which the innocent appeal. This is the moral doctrine with which we inoculate our newly made citizens, and under which the children of our overcrowded tenement houses grow up. As the boys approach manhood they know no greater privilege than to serve the man who has the power to give them place, and he begins to cultivate their acquaintance early.

It takes brains, moral standards, a knowledge of life and experience to put the district leaders and their cohorts in the place they belong. Talking against them accomplishes nothing while the majority he represents keeps him in power, yes, makes him possible. He makes morality an evil, dishonesty justice to the people who know him as the representative of republican principles. They are the people. They have left one land because it deprived them of rights. Rights as they know

MEETING THE NEEDS OF THE NEIGHBORHOOD.

them are personal, and the district leader secures them.

The opposition to the reform movement by the people governed by the district leader comes from the conviction, dimly conceived or implanted, that the election of the men who represent it would mean that everywhere merit and not "pull" would keep the voter at work; that business would have to be conducted according to law; that crime would be punished; that no man would hold the keys of the prison for their benefit, but for the protection of the community.

One of the greatest moral lessons administered to the people of New York in a language that all understood, and one which all classes in the community needed, was given by the late Colonel George E. Waring. When he organized the Department of Street Cleaning on the merit system; when he proved to every man in the department that if he did his work no man could displace him; that he could defend himself, a man before men, if charges were brought against him, Colonel Waring changed the moral character of New York. Every man in that department had his friends to whom he carried the message; stood a free man employed by the city; a man who dared to vote as he would though in public service;

would not be deprived of the right to earn his daily bread because of the use he made of his rights as an American citizen. This moral lesson went into every home. The woman whose husband handled a broom, drove a cart, held her head up, for the magic D. S. C. had changed a "job" that enslaved her husband to an employment that honored him.

The enforcement of the law in the gathering of the garbage; the cleanliness of the streets in the tenement-house districts equal to those of the avenues, for the first time in generations brought the great truth to the consciousness of the people in the tenement-house regions that all men were equal. That the clean streets led to clean halls and cleaner homes was natural; and the further evolution meant clean characters, because of moral freedom to express opinion in a ballot cast at no man's command.

And then came the summers when, for the sake of the children, extra exertions were made to keep the streets clean. Slowly the truth dawned on the dullest mother that the babies were not dying in such numbers; were not so ill, because the streets were clean, the garbage collected and the streets washed and cool. Twenty years of Colonel Waring, and the moral tone of the most ignorant would be changed. For the right to earn his living honestly, honorably, to cast his ballot as an American citizen, would be guaranteed to every voter employed in a city department employing the greatest number of voters with the least manual ability, the least education.

A city is just as honest as the greatest number of citizens casting a ballot with the least knowledge of its value and effect; it comes no higher in the scale of integrity than that. Every man who stands behind a broom because he earns what is paid him, and knows that he stays there just as long as he continues to earn his wages, represents a wealth of manhood in a democracy, a part of the nation's capital as a world power.

When Colonel Waring discharged the first man convicted of accepting a bribe for collecting the refuse of the city contrary to the law of the department, he gave a practical demonstration of the truth of the Declaration of Independence that all men are born free and equal. He showed by that act that the poor man who could not pay a bribe was protected by the law; that wealth purchased no privileges at the expense of the city. Just where the spoils system had worked its deepest degradation it received its most effective lesson. The greatest benefit that Colonel Waring, that man of law and order, conferred upon New York, was not its clean streets, but the moral lesson that a city department can be administered to secure the best interests of the people on the principles that control the best business houses of the city.

To the shame of the city be it said that it had so long been accustomed to the spoils system that it could not accept the theory of Colonel Waring. It was impossible for even the philanthropic workers to believe that a man would not be placed, if they used their personal "pull" with the head of the department. The politicians learned quickly that the system in that department ignored "pull." When they did accept it, they determined to overthrow the man who robbed the spoils system of its largest perquisite where it was most effective in numbers. The combination of the political machines accomplished the city's disgrace in 1897. It was redeemed in 1901 by a people who had suffered cruelly; who saw in the four years of misrule that they had made their own chains of bondage.

CHAPTER III.

THE HOMES UNDER ONE ROOF.

THE importance of environment is at last admitted as a factor in character-building. That light and air are indispensable to cleanliness, and physical cleanliness to health, and health to morals, is the gospel that the evils of the tenements have forced the philanthropists to declare until the thinking public is convinced of its truth.

There are tenement houses that have reputations as positive as individuals. Thoughtful, intelligent wives of workingmen would not, could not be persuaded to move into them because of their reputations. Often the evils of these tenements are justly attributed to the housekeepers. Housekeepers of tenements are women who pay the whole or a part of their rent by overseeing the house; attending to the cleaning, collecting the rents, letting the rooms, adjusting differences between tenants—"a go-between" between the agent or the owner and the tenants. The owner or agent employing these women upholds their decisions when differences between the tenants and housekeepers arise. This clothes them with great authority, and often enables them to do great injustice. They are feared usually. Families will endure restrictions of liberties, every deprivation of their rights, because protest would mean eviction or discomforts that would compel them to move.

Under some agents and owners these housekeepers have absolute control of the property. They frequently make and enforce rules that utterly ignore the rights of tenants. This rule is often as absolute as though they were the owners of the house. Strange as it may seem, this class of housekeepers usually make the property under their control pay; they usually keep up the character of the houses under their control because they have standards and compel those about them to live up to them.

On an East Side street a few blocks from the East River are four 27-foot front houses of the English-basement type. The plan of these houses indicates that they were designed as residences for people of ample means. The halls are broad, the stairways wide, ascending in recesses on the first floor that leaves the entrance halls clear from front to rear doorways. The yards of these four houses, wide and deep, are paved with broad flagging stones, such as are used on the sidewalks.

A REMNANT OF THE PAST.

The fences are kept in good order and well painted. Not a child living in these four houses dares to play in those yards. The housekeeper—one woman has charge of the four houses—would order them out. If the children did not leave at once, complaint would be made to the mothers; and if they did not uphold the housekeeper and insist that the children play in the street, the mothers who failed would have to move. Every mother-tenant knows this well. A mother of three children who had lived in these houses all her married life, when asked why the children could not play in the yard, where she could watch them, replied: "Why, if the children played in the yard they would make a lot of work for the housekeeper. She would not stand it." This mother's tone indicated that she thought the housekeeper was right. The youngest of the three children in another family living in these houses was ill all winter. When convalescent, the doctor ordered him to be kept out of doors as much as possible. The mother had all the work to do for five in family, and had to devise some means of keeping the child out that would not interfere with her work. She arranged the fire-escape outside of the window, putting pillows and toys out there. The little fellow climbed over the rail and struck a stone beneath, breaking his arms.

"Why did you not put him in the yard, where you could watch him, and where he could run about?"

"Oh! the housekeeper would be so angry; I wouldn't dare."

"Must you keep the children out of the yard?"

"Yes; they would make an awful lot of work for the housekeeper."

Investigation proved that the owner of this property supported the housekeeper in depriving even the babies of the use of these yards. A mother could not roll a baby carriage around the yards, because her older children, if she had any, would be sure to go into the yards to see her. The rents for four rooms, two absolutely dark, ventilated through the dark and unventilated halls by a window eighteen inches square, were $22, $20 and $18 per month, respectively, for each floor. The streets in front are overcrowded, dirty; when the trucks were in the streets, two were always standing in front of these houses. Push-carts now replace the trucks.

The people stay in these houses year after year. A bill never appears on them. The arbitrary restriction as to the use of the yard is not counted against the property, because it is so clean, kept in such good repair, and the character of the people scrutinized before they are accepted as tenants. It is generally understood that the renting of furnished rooms is not approved. The housekeeper finds a tenant who rents rooms objectionable. In a neighborhood where every house shows year after year a loss of character, people poorer and more ignorant becoming tenants, these four houses retain the appearance of comfort and respectability. Among the tenants there is but little intimacy; they appear to have little in common. The women are never heard in the halls, nor do they loiter about the doorways. The men are all skilled workmen, earning good wages—clerks on small salaries, or in city departments, all natives of New York. The wives were all wage-earners before they were married. They dress well; most of them are fairly good housekeepers. All buy their children's clothes ready made; two make their own dresses. For their children they are ambitious, and expect to keep them in school until they are sixteen. This the children defeat. The boys get places during the summer vacations in their fourteenth year, refusing to go back to school. The girls are contented until fourteen, and then they grow restless, becoming wage-earners; all that they earn is spent for their clothes. The wages of the father may no more than meet the expenses of the family, but this is not considered. Clothes are the essentials.

A man having a salary of $1,400, living in one of these houses, had to go in debt the first week of a serious illness of his wife. He did not have a dollar in advance to meet emergencies. He was a proud, indulgent, tender husband and father.

This type of house and this class of tenants are disappearing from the East Side. The remnant of this class who remain are held by political affiliations or family ties. The men enjoy the sense of power that comes from this connection, and realize fully that to leave the district would mean a loss of social prestige, or, if minor politicians, a loosening of their hold on the people to whom they represent political power. Many of this class remain in the section because they hold positions in the city departments in return for active service in the interest of the political machines.

Not far away from these tenements is another in which are sixteen families. The rents in this house range from $5 to $9.50 per month for two to three rooms. The house is dirty, neglected; violations of the sanitary laws are evident from the front door to the roof, on which tenants occupying the front rooms must dry their clothes. The water is in the dark halls; in winter, for days at a time, the pipes, both water and drain, are frozen and burst; yet the tenants stay year after year. One woman, the mother of four children, was born, married, her four children were born, and her husband, mother and father died in this house. She has never moved, except across the hall, up and downstairs, as she has been able to pay more or has been forced to reduce her rent. The women in this house know almost nothing of housekeeping. The men are employed only about half the time. The number of children in the house averages three to each family. It is a New England hamlet under one roof in this particular. If there is sickness in any family, it is the concern of every tenant; if a man is out of work, it is a community misfortune, and to be shared. A new hat for man or woman is the cause of rejoicing, for it is the badge of respectability for any in the house who may need it in an emergency. The whole household, for such it seems to be, are poor, very poor; thriftless, unambitious; the men somewhat given to drink to excess; yet the spirit of neighborliness shames criticism. A woman in this house ill four months was nursed by her neighbors night and day. Her house and children were cared for, food provided when necessary. Comment on their loyalty and devotion was met with the response: "God knows how soon she may be doing it for one of us." Yet when that woman, whom most of them had known all her life, gave evidence of pregnancy a few months after her husband's death, not a woman crossed her doorsill until the birth of twin babies within the period of time redeemed her character. Whether from remorse or love, ample return for this cruelty has been made many times.

In the two-room apartments in this house there is one closet, with shelves about six inches wide. This is in the one room that serves as living-room, kitchen, dining-room—a room less than eight feet wide. The bedroom is perfectly dark, ventilated by a square window into perfectly dark, unventilated halls. A full-sized bed leaves the width of the door between it and the wall. The three-room apartments have outside windows—five to the three rooms. There is a closet in the kitchen and one in the large room. People talk of poverty, but few people know what it is. A woman who had moved into the three-room apartment had hung all the clothing for five in family in the one bedroom on four nails. In reply to a protest, she said patiently and quietly: "There are no hooks in the closet in the front room, and I hadn't a penny to buy any." Ten cents provided that closet with hooks. A comment was made on the keeping of the washtub under the kitchen table. "Why do you not have the tub carried to the cellar?" An expression of self-pity passed over the woman's face as she explained that the tub would have to be carried down three flights of stairs, out on the street, around the corner, down the cellar stairs, and then to her coal cellar at the extreme end of the cellar.

The house stands on a corner, the entrance from the street at the extreme end of the west wall. The cellar door was formerly close to the entrance door, but the landlord built in the back end of the cellar an oven when a baker hired the store on the first floor. A cellar door was then opened at the farthest part of the front, or south wall, one hundred and twenty-five feet from the entrance door of the house. Is it surprising that coal is bought by the pail by all the tenants? That tubs are kept anywhere in their rooms where there is space?

Shiftlessness, thriftless uncleanliness marks even the sidewalk about this house. The dirt inside or out troubles nobody. Children will spill half the contents of the garbage pail they are carrying to the cans in the tiny yard, in halls and on the stairway. It is kicked out of the way without comment. Dogs or cats, and ofttimes both, are members of the families who live under this roof. The unsanitary conditions of the closets in the yard arouse pity for the tenants on the first floor; but no tenant thinks of complaining to either the housekeeper or the authorities. It would be useless, and would get them into trouble. The present owner is willing to kalsomine the bedrooms and halls each spring, but the tenants object because it makes a lot of work.

In August, two years ago, the writer was going up the first flight of stairs in this house, when a baby voice was heard pleading: "Pease tum fas'er; oh, pease tum fas'er; I 'ant to do p'ay; I 'ant to doe on steet; pease tum fas'er." On the third floor a tiny boy stood in front of the sink talking to the faucet, from which a tiny stream was flowing into a little tin pail. An infant's voice from one of the rooms told the story. The mother needed water and could not leave the baby. Perhaps this was the tiny nurse of mother and baby, big enough to call a neighbor to do what he could not do.

When it is remembered that this stream of water from the faucet represented the water supply for four families, the difficulties of cleanliness under those conditions may be slightly appreciated. In spite of the dirt, the darkness, the unsanitary conditions of this house, the thriftlessness and ignorance of the tenants, there is a spirit of neighborliness in it that puts the critical to blush. Without a doubt the housekeeper, who is a shrewd woman, fosters this spirit of neighborliness. She smiles as she says: "They gets so used to each other they hates to be separated." Neither house nor tenants seem to go below the level established twelve years ago.

There is a housekeeper who does mission work of which the world takes no note. She is the woman who in the true sense is an altruist. By her force of character, her hatred of inefficiency, her love of order, she compels the women who become tenants who do not know how to keep house to learn how.

The writer knows intimately such a housekeeper. She had charge of a four-story tenement on the lower East Side. The house was of the type known as "double decker." There were four apartments on each floor; the front consisting of a kitchen, living-room and two bedrooms; the back, of one room and two bedrooms. Small windows near the ceiling in kitchen and bedrooms opened on a narrow space between this and the next house, which was an old-fashioned residence. A similar opening in that house enabled the neighbors to look into each other's rooms. Water and refuse were thrown into this space between the two houses, and sometimes into the rooms of neighbors unintentionally. There was war, bitter war, because of this; for the large tenement was occupied by a part of the remnant having social standards left on the lower East Side.

There was water in all the kitchens of the large tenement. The halls were absolutely dark, but were free from the nuisances of hallways having sinks. Stairs and halls were covered with light oilcloth, the stairs having brass treads on the edge. Everything was kept as clean as soap, water and muscular strength could keep it.

The first visit was made to this house long before Colonel Waring had shown what clean streets would do in the tenement-house districts. On the street curb in front of the door stood three ash barrels filled within three inches of the top, carefully covered with newspapers tucked in around the edge of the contents. This indicates the standards of this housekeeper. She hated dirt and disorder. She could not be happy where it was. She forced by tact, coercion, persuasion, any and every means, her way to the heart and home of every ignorant housekeeper who came under that roof. She taught cooking by sending cake, bread, soup she had made to the tenants, and arousing the desire in them to learn how to make that particular dish. She instituted an exchange of skill among the tenants. The woman who could make a dress and not a hat exchanged skill with the one who had been a milliner. The woman who made bread and failed with cake exchanged skill with the cakemaker. They even took turns in going to the theatre, the neighbor staying home and taking care of the children.

The property was more valuable every year; no bill appeared at the door. It stood apart from its neighbors for years. This housekeeper was compelled to give up her responsibility and left the house, as she wisely said: "No one would manage it in my way. I could not get on in peace." Six months after every tenant had moved but the liquor dealer; and even his barroom had sunk to a lower level. A building in which many homes might be maintained is now merely a place of shelter. People move in and out; no relations are established; there is nothing to hold the tenant here above any other house. The owner has sold the property, hating its present character.

Again, tenants will be the victims of vindictive housekeepers, who for any and no reason will begin a system of petty persecutions to compel a tenant to move. Then there is the gossiping housekeeper, who keeps the tenants at war. It is no secret that the method of rent collecting of some housekeepers holds tenants year after year. They will take the rent in the smallest sums, daily or weekly. By the end of the month they will usually have the full amount collected. The houses where this system prevails are the most objectionable. The tenants for this leniency endure positive evils. The important thing is a place of shelter for the family. Work is uncertain, or long periods of idleness has made the payment of rent impossible for a period. The housekeeper understands and becomes responsible for keeping the tenant until the rent is paid. In return the tenants endure neglect of duty on the part of the housekeeper. Silence is their expression of gratitude. No repairs are made, for none are demanded. The house sinks lower and lower; anybody can move in on the payment of part of a month's rent. The vacant rooms are dirty—give visible evidence of the presence of vermin; but the family evicted with only half a month's rent in hand cannot afford to be critical. This is the house that makes the slum.

Two housekeepers of tenements were discussing owners and tenants before the writer. One was rigid, keeping the house astonishingly clean, with rooms rarely vacant; the other, always in trouble with the tenants, always having some one to evict, threw the blame for her troubles on the tenants. The first one listened, finally saying slowly: "No, you are the one. You get cross and abuse the children. You make pets of some chil-

A TYPE OF THE PRESENT.

dren and some mothers, and the others see it and get mad. Then there is a fight. To keep a house you must treat everybody the same. You must make good rules; you must do your part and make every tenant do her part. I've had two of the tenants you put out of your house five years. They are good tenants; watch yourself."

There are landlords who care for nothing but the income from their property. Any kind of tenant who will pay rent is acceptable. Any housekeeper who collects the specified amount may hold control without question. The housekeeper may have standards, but these are swept aside by the exactions of the landlord. The rents in such houses are usually high, because there is such a percentage of loss in rents. This house also contributes to the creation of the slum.

The careless and apparently malicious destruction of property by tenants is not appreciated by those who touch this question of tenement houses superficially. No means has yet been found to make the tenement-house population understand that the abuse of property is a factor in their rent problem. Within a year the writer was walking with a group of women, two of whom were housekeepers in tenement houses. This question of tenants was being discussed freely by the women who were tenants as well as the housekeepers.

It was interesting to find that all agreed that one family could change the character of a tenement house for the worst, but one family could not improve its character. The reason was that the family above the tenement came only to reduce their rent during a hard time, while the family with evil tendencies stayed until they were put out, to go into a cheaper tenement and lower that. They agreed that where housekeeper and tenant got on well together both hated a change. The two things that dragged down the character of a tenement was beer-drinking and destructive children—children allowed to "run wild." These women insisted that there never would be quarrels in tenement houses were it not for these two causes. A woman who drank beer would invite her new neighbors to drink. They would treat in return, and the house would show it at once. The women who drink beer in this fashion grow careless of their persons and their homes; they get rid of their children, who soon learn to enjoy the freedom from control. The children destroy the property first in play, through carelessness, and later grow malicious.

If a housekeeper is sharp and shrewd, these women tenants claimed that she could at any time get rid of an objectionable tenant; but the housekeepers held that if the owner did not care for anything but rents, the housekeeper was often compelled to let in and keep in objectionable tenants. They admitted, one and all, that houses fairly indicated the character of the people who would live in them, and that rents regulated the class of tenants to a very great degree. They admitted that at times one could find tenants who had lived for many years in one house where conditions had changed for the worst. But it was unusual. People now selected houses where those of their own faith, and, if foreign, those of their own nationality, at least predominated. That this tendency was seen more and more every year. This group of women were among the remnant of Christians left on the lower East Side. All had been born there of Irish parentage. They lived in the houses bordering on the edge of the East River—old houses on the plan of the first tenements erected in New York, or in houses designed for one family and now holding four to eight. Two of them lived in houses built in a row erected eighty-three years ago. They were two-story, dormer windows and basement frame houses, built without an area, the door to the basements opening like a cellar door on the street. These basements were occupied by a family each. Fourteen of these houses are still standing. The people in this section live a life entirely their own.

They have been crowded out, the more prosperous, by the Hebrews, while the remnant find themselves hemmed in by them.

These people live in the confines of a Roman Catholic parish that twenty years ago contained nearly eleven thousand souls of that faith. Three years ago the priest in charge estimated his parish at less than four thousand, and that four thousand remained because they were too poor to get away, he declared.

The Hebrews, as tenants will, on the same block show many social grades, many degrees of poverty and prosperity, many stages of development in American civilization. There is a sense of feeling of brotherhood that other people lack. The houses will range from the most uncleanly, ill-kept, to the new tenement with ornate entrance and modern improvements. The most modern will, on entering, be found with walls marked and broken when the wood-work is new. No one seems troubled by this destruction. The housekeeper does not struggle, for it is expected and charged for in the rent. Plumbing is of the simplest, for it is expected to present the largest percentage of loss in the administration of the property. One of the most elaborate of the new tenements erected on the lower East Side was visited three months after it was occupied. Every hallway from top to bottom of the house had broken plaster and was marked by pencil and crayon. The plumber was then a daily visitor. This house a year afterward bore on the interior evidences that years of hard usage might have brought. The housekeeper collected rents and attended to the garbage. She was utterly indifferent to the appearance of the house, which, intended for prosperous families, was a nest of sweat-shops, where even children of six and seven were employed. The rents had been collected; that was the owner's only requirement.

The West Side is congested, because manufacture and storehouses are displacing the houses. Rents are high, and the houses for the most part old residences occupied by several families. The people, generally, are Americans. They are deeply attached to this old section, because it is their birthplace; and for many of them an even deeper attachment prevails, for this section was the birthplace of parents. The houses often are found to have life-long friends, often relatives, as tenants. The tenants keep the halls and stairways clean in turn, and the houses generally are well kept up. Here one tenant is allowed a rebate on rent for renting rooms, collecting the rent, caring for the sidewalk and stoop, the garbage and ash-cans. The majority of the people in this section are

Protestants. The Protestant churches are well maintained. The Trinity Corporation supports kindergartens, cooking and sewing schools. The Judson Memorial is a very attractive gymnasium, that brings children from as far west as the North River. The Methodist Church holds many who in no other section could find the same equality and freedom. The vocabulary of the people through this section shows the effect of the newer activities in the modern churches; the effect of the enlarging interests of the children in art and nature through the public school education.

While the people are living on small incomes, often on uncertain incomes, life is lived at a much higher level than on the East Side. Children are not so precocious in evil knowledge. This difference is due largely to the fact that the houses contain three and four families at the most; that the apartment houses in the section are beyond the reach of any but the skilled working man. He holds his own at high rental in the house that shelters but three other families like his own. His neighbors are people of like ambitions as his own, and demand what he demands.

The housekeepers in this section differ essentially in their relation to the tenants from those of the more heterogeneous population of the East Side of the city. One resemblance is recog-

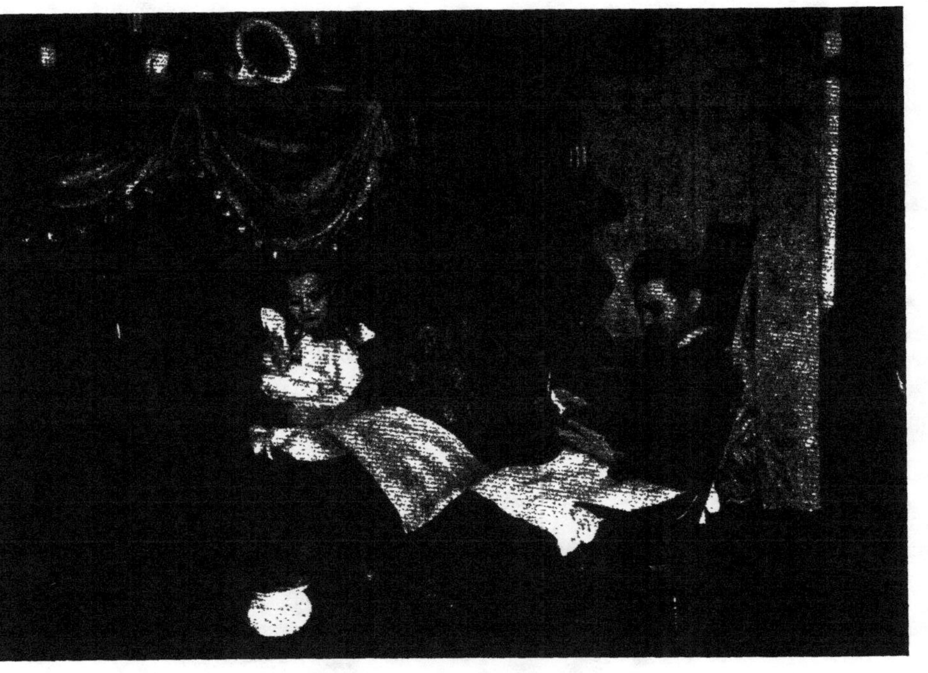

A CORNER IN A WORKINGMAN'S HOME.

nized—the effect of the character of the housekeeper. Here, as on the East Side, to a very large degree, the comfort, health, peace and goodwill of the tenants in every house depends on the character and the spirit of the woman who controls the property for the landlord.

The law of natural selection holds good. The housekeeper holds the tenants who are satisfied with the conditions she creates. They, especially the children, develop in habits of cleanliness, in care of property, in respect for the rights of others, as the rules of the house enforced by the housekeeper compel. It is in her power to get rid of those who do not accept her dictates, let them be what they may—just or unjust. The housekeeper will make her presence felt. If she violates the law in the disposal of garbage outside of the house, tenants will violate the law she makes for them in the care and disposal of garbage inside the house. If she is compelled to obey the law, she will compel tenants to obey the law. It is this that makes the morale of the Department of Street Cleaning so important. If the part of the house which in renting tenants agree to keep clean is not kept clean, the observer will discover that the housekeeper does not keep her part of the agreement in keeping the entrance clean.

A large factor in the tenement house for character building or destroying is the housekeeper who has charge of it. Where she is well paid she makes the property valuable. She cares for it, for the character of the tenants. Tenants remain in the house because of the advantages her offices control for the poor man and his wife anxious to provide for their children's best welfare. Property under this type of woman resists decay. She holds it in spite of the decay about it. The characterless, slovenly, indifferent housekeeper is a factor in destroying property, because of the destructive character of the tenants who will tolerate her and her methods.

The house that is the property of the man with "a pull" is an obstruction to civilization almost impossible to overcome. By connivance the law is inoperative. If pushed, such an owner can easily rid himself of the tenants who attempt, or have attempted for them, efforts to compel the owners to repair the property. A mill owner on the water front on the lower East Side owned three three-story and basement houses adjoining the mill property. They had been built for one family each. The basements were altered into stores, and the floors above altered at the least cost to accommodate one or two families. This meant two inside bedrooms absolutely without ventilation. The tenants of this property and all in the neighborhood were tormented by the smoke and gas from the chimney of the mill. When the wind blew directly toward the houses, windows were kept closed for hours in the warmest weather. All the tenants dried their clothes on pulley lines. Frequently the soot made the clothes unwearable, and they had to be washed the second time. Ten years of effort have failed to compel the building of the chimney of that mill to the legal height.

The houses the mill owner owned were in a disgraceful condition. The closets in the yards had no flow of water. The engineer of the mill was required to carry a hose from the mill over the fences to the closets to flush them. Sometimes he forgot to turn the water off, and the yards were flooded and made disgusting. Sometimes he forgot for days at a time to flush the closets, when the conditions were even worse. Only people who were helpless or hopeless would endure such conditions. One of the workers of the College Settlement discovered the conditions in these houses. She took immediate steps to compel the necessary improvements. The owner discovered that the wife and children of one of the tenants went to clubs at the Settlement, and he ordered that family to move. Before the mother moved her education had begun, and she imparted to her neighbors the information that the conditions were unlawful and could be changed if they would fight for it. The man exacted his rent on the first of the month; he was hard and unyielding; the tenants continued the warfare until he had evicted every one who spoke English and filled his houses with foreigners. One of the stores is used for storing and sorting rags and paper; next door is a meat shop. The fight was given up. The owner had "a pull," and the law is defied to this day on that property.

All the land on the river front in this neighborhood for blocks is made land, filled in by the city refuse, on which houses were built years ago. This kind of property extends back from the North River for three, and at one point four, blocks. In some of the houses near the river the high tides of spring and fall rise in the cellars. The College Settlement workers who visited families in one of these houses had been distressed by the amount of illness in it. Malaria had attacked every family. Spring and fall wages were lost at times by as many as three wage-earners in one family for two and three days each week. In addition to loss of wages, there was the expense of medicine and doctors. At last came the urgent request that a worker should call on a girl of sixteen who was dying of consumption on the first floor. This consisted of four rooms, two being inside bedrooms, each of which would hold a three-quarter bed and a chair between the bed and the wall. One was absolutely unventilated, except through the doors. It was, in fact, a passage-way between the front and rear rooms. This plan is the usual plan in houses altered from residences for one family to a tenement house.

The door of the other bedroom, which opened into the large room, was closed at night because the large room was used as a bedroom by the male members of the family and one lodger. The girl of sixteen had slept with two others in that room for eight years. The floors of the four rooms were covered with carpets. The odor was sickening. The visitor asked the tenant who brought her to the sick girl what caused the odor perceptible in the hall, with front and rear windows always open, unbearable in the rooms where doors and windows were closed.

"Oh, that! The water has been in the cellar now for two or three weeks. The tides are high now." A visit to the cellar showed the water at the height of the second step of the cellar stairs; also a sewer pipe that had burst. Visits were made to the proper city department once a week for eleven weeks. The clerk, on the last visit, evidently intending to be facetious, said: "Say, what's the matter with those people taking baths in that cellar? They ain't got no bathtubs."

The owner of the property had "pull" enough to escape even an investigation by the department. It was years before the cellar of that house was concreted and the necessary connections of pipes and sewers made. It was done when the property had changed hands and a man comparatively poor and wholly free from political affiliations became the owner.

The people of this whole region are the victims of political corruption. Some of them have more fear of offending a political light, let his glimmer be ever so small, than of offending against even God's law. They could be turned out of house and home, deprived of the means of earning a living, by men who openly defy the law, and who become heroes to the growing boys and girls for no reason but because of their power to use and defy the law.

The moral natures of the men and the women who grow up under this influence are dwarfed and warped until it is impossible for them to have distinct conceptions of right and wrong. The education they receive does not reveal the relations of ethics to life; the struggle for existence dulls the mind; while the depleted physical conditions caused by bad air, mal-nutrition and ignorance of real values reduce moral resistance almost to zero. Enforce the tenement-house laws, and the moral strength of the people of New York will rise to higher levels of moral resistance. Not poverty, but the burden imposed by political corruption, is the blight of home life in the tenement-house sections of New York.

CHAPTER IV.

SLOW-DAWNING CONSCIOUSNESS.

In a preceding chapter an attempt was made to show how hopeless the task of home-making was for women who had neither knowledge nor ideals to guide them. When it is remembered that the environment of these homes was in itself degrading, to maintain even the semblance of a home was a remarkable achievement.

These women knew but three educating influences—home, school and Church. Four, perhaps, if one chooses to count the streets, where most of their time was spent, as one. The value of the first they revealed in the homes they made. The school at the time it was a factor in their development was a place that had no connection with anything else in their lives. What they learned there was but to the exceptional few without any practical value. They learned to read to get promoted, or because they could not help it. The arithmetic which they found valuable they learned in doing errands and spending their own pennies. They learned to form letters with their pens; but as they had no use for the knowledge, they soon forgot it. Their conception of education and that of their world left them perfectly at ease in their accomplishment. The Church had to do with their souls; and to the majority the care of their souls was a delegated responsibility, and gave them little concern, if any. Personal effort in that direction was a matter of old age.

The Church was, by its own traditions and sentiment, a spiritual light and guide; the end and aim of its service to develop spiritual life by teaching and prayer. The social life of the people, or, for that matter, the civic conditions that to the last degree regulated and controlled their pleasures, were not the concern of the Church. The parish house did not exist. The institutional church had not been conceived even in thought.

Yet at this period, 1880 and 1881, there was a growing consciousness that something was wrong in the social order; that neither churches, schools nor homes were meeting the necessities of the working people or their children. The Church found itself losing ground; the people could not be held in allegiance to it. This was so true of the Protestant churches downtown that already the wisdom of moving uptown was being questioned. Some had even then left their old buildings to be used as mission churches; others sold their downtown buildings, moving uptown, giving up any attempt at holding the masses, who manifested no interest in the Church or its work. The missions then established were and are maintained with more or less wisdom and success. That mistakes should be made was natural. There was no precedent as to how one class in this democratic community should work for another. It took years for the churches to learn that the secret of success was in working *with,* and not *for,* the people.

The overcrowding went on. Neighborhoods changed so rapidly that it was impossible to adopt any system to meet the necessities of the social conditions. These conditions were created by race standards of living, pleasure and religion. No man or organization was prepared to grapple with them intelligently, for they viewed them as observers.

The Church had still the first interpretation of feeding the hungry, clothing the naked, visiting the sick and those in prison. Secular work was not yet a part of the redemptive work of the Church. Poverty and ignorance reigned where prosperity and intelligence had been. The mission church became a distributing station. It was but natural that the men and women who followed Christ in their lives should feed and clothe

the hungry and the naked. It was quite as natural that people whose struggle for life was constant, a struggle in which they were rarely successful, even when they accepted their own standards of success, should develop shrewdness in securing all possible aid at the least possible effort. The more they received without effort, the easier life was made for them. This was one method of adjustment. Where there were several children in a family they were often sent to as many Sunday-schools. The churches, all unconsciously, for a long period carried on the work of the missions on a commercial basis, competing energetically to secure attendants at mission services and Sunday-schools. The workers found their success measured by the numbers that appeared in their reports. It was the American standard of success. It became profitable to go to Sunday-school. The approach of the holidays found them crowded. The mission churches boomed. They provided an outlet for the energies of devoted, consecrated men and women, determined to make the world better because they were in it. The missions were an outlet for the generous; for the men and the women who considered themselves stewards of the properties in their possession. The blunders made are a tribute to the faith which established and maintained churches. The very blunders of those years were the seeds of wisdom these latter days are beginning to garner in the fruits of coöperation and federation. The forces are beginning to marshal under one banner and emblem, with one aim born of the nineteenth century conception, that Christ taught civic duty to His followers when He declared, "Render unto Cæsar the things that are Cæsar's." That the Church is the guardian of the people's rights, as well as their example, is a long-delayed conception. It has taken thirty years to bring the evolution in Church work from competition to coöperation in the work of personal and civic regeneration.

Many of the difficulties hardest to overcome have grown out of the mistakes of those years, when the rapid influx of foreigners changed the character of the people of the tenement regions, and the Church failed to change its methods. They came, many of them, paupers, a charge at once upon the charitable and the humane. Neither their ignorance nor poverty was a bar to their citizenship; their presence on the municipal stage in the character of voters, sovereigns, increased the civic problems of New York, and naturally these the Church problems.

Unfortunately the charitable work of the churches was too often left to the management of sentimental people, who failed to see what has been forced upon workers of the present day: that hunger is sometimes a moral educator; that the salvation of a family may sometimes be best secured by letting them suffer, the innocent with the guilty, because in the suffering is an educating power impossible to secure in any other way.

One evening to a working-girls' club a teacher in a mission school not far away brought a girl of sixteen, introducing her as one of her girls who had been in her class two years. Privately she told one of the directors of the club of the poverty of the girl's family. The father was a man of seventy-five, who could do only the lightest work, and found getting the work he could do very difficult. This girl was the eldest of seven children, all attending the mission. "It is a mystery what would become of the family, were it not for what the mission does for them," was the comment of the teacher. A close inspection of the girl did not reveal distressing poverty, and the directors of the club were puzzled. The girl was employed in a store at a very small salary. She was anxious to go to the country. Of course, she must be sent away without any cost to herself. She doubted if the family could spare her wages, even if she could go free. She explained that she and her brothers and sisters had gone in

"Tribune Fresh-Air Parties," but she was now too old. "The trouble with our family is," she commented, "that we are all too old." It seemed a hopeless doctrine to become fixed in the mind of a girl of sixteen, so the club directors secured a vacation for her through the Working-Girls' Vacation Society, deciding that, if it were necessary, they would pay the mother her wages for the time the girl was away. No question arose as to her wages. At the expiration of her two weeks' vacation, when she should have been penniless, she appeared at the club in a new hat and gloves. When the girl joined the club her Sunday-school teacher paid one month's dues. She had been present at several business meetings; she had seen the other girls paying their dues, she had heard the treasurer's report, but she never attempted to assume her financial obligations. She was spoken to finally in regard to her dues, and responded calmly by saying she could not pay her dues; she had no money. Various suggestions were made as to the possibility of her paying part. At last, to relieve the club treasury, one of the directors said: "I will pay what you owe and one month in advance. You may pay me as you can." The girl never came to the club again. No effort was made to trace her, as she contributed nothing to the life of the club, and many girls kept their dues paid who dressed far more plainly; these very girls she had on more than one occasion treated discourteously.

Two years afterward one of the club officers was calling on a friend. "I am so glad you came in," she exclaimed. "One of your club girls is in trouble and is coming here with Miss ——, a mission worker in Dr. ——'s church, this morning. Now you can help solve her problem." To have a member of a working-girls' club go to an outsider for help is to have one of your own family appeal to strangers in time of need. The club worker kept still. She was covered with shame. She had failed to establish relations with one it was her sole purpose to help. Who the girl was she did not know, as her friend had forgotten the girl's name. The girl came. It was our old friend of sixteen. She was, as may be imagined, not pleased to see the director of the club. The history of that family is fairly indicative of how missions were conducted at that time. How many of them are conducted at the present with the same results? Originally this family was found by the workers of a mission established by a wealthy church, and apparently in need. Rent was paid; food and clothes provided; doctors sent when necessary. The return for this, as tacitly agreed, was the presence of the children, as rapidly as they were old enough, in the Sunday-school, and the father and mother at the Sunday evening service, the only service this mission maintained.

The timidity of the first contact disappeared early. The wants soon outgrew the needs of the family. The mission people failed to respond to the wants, and watched more closely what it cost the church to meet the needs after the first years of acquaintance. This was not to be borne. The family went in a body to another mission of the same church ten blocks away. They made not the slightest effort to deceive, for they did not change their address. Here were nine persons to add to the roll of the mission, and they were added. The family was enthusiastically welcomed. No impudent or intrusive questions were asked. Shoes, coats, rent money in whole or part was generously given. At the end of two years discoveries were made that led the mission workers to question what was done with the supplies provided. The family would not stand this. They went bodily to a church less than a mile away, still living at the old address. The family was again taken up without question. That the father could not work was accepted and generosity was increased. The other missions contrasted unfavorably in generous impulses; the girl urged her former classmates to join the last mission. The church meanwhile was walking by faith in its treatment of the poor; aiming to live up to the conception of its days; strengthening the influence of its prayers with gifts of potatoes; certainly a great advance on prayers and no potatoes.

At about this time a young girl was met in a Sunday-school class very attractive, always well and prettily dressed. She had been in the Sunday-school all her life, and had joined the church with her mother, a gentle, quiet woman, who leaned on her daughter for guidance. The daughter was a tower of strength. By accident it was learned that the girl was a wage-earner, working with her mother in a large suit house in New York; that they kept house, doing the housework, even the washing and ironing, before and after their day's work. Added to this they made all their own clothes, which must have involved a vast amount of labor, as they both dressed well.

The position of this mother and daughter is fairly typical of a large army of women workers, and explains, in part, at least, why two women of so much character should have accepted charity for so many years and why they could not change their economic relation. The work they did was to a degree a trade. Each was a special "hand" on a certain part of women's suits. They were paid by the piece. When they had work, they made good wages; but the seasons were short. The beginning of every season found them in debt. By the time the debt was paid work had grown slack or stopped. It was simply impossible to get beyond this, try as they would. When the girl broke down, she explained it by saying, "I worked all night to finish my dress. If I could buy the material in the slack season I could make our things then. We never have the money, and they have to be made just when work is hardest at the store." She was but nineteen. The girl was pretty, ambitious, entirely above the men of her own station in refinement, and yet quite as far beneath the brothers of the girls she met in her Sunday-school class. She lived in mental terror lest they should attempt to call on her. It was pitiful to see the struggle she made to conceal the fact that she was poor. The other girls knew she worked, knew the church helped the family, but were very tactful in assisting her in keeping her secret.

When the mother came to the notice of the officers of the church she was a widow with three young children, one a baby. She could support her family if the rent was paid. The church officers were glad to do this. They did not support a mission and had very little outlet for the church's generosity, except the mission societies —Home and Foreign—to which they were devoted as a church.

For thirteen years the church had been faithful to its promise and paid the rent. Nobody questioned the mother as to how her children were getting on, or what was being done to make them self-supporting. The younger were two boys. When they were large enough to play on the street, the mother put them in an institution and paid a small sum for them. The girl went to work with the mother as soon as she could. The elder boy came home at fourteen and became a wage-earner. He was troublesome, most difficult to manage, was out of work more time than he was employed, and yet he would not when unemployed even keep the fire, that the house might be comfortable when his mother and sister came home. They always left the house in order when they went to work, but found it littered when they returned. The boy had no sense of moral responsibility for his own support. His temper was wholly untrained. At the time the family history was connected, the youngest boy was to come home, and naturally his return was dreaded. The mother and daughter met the problem unaided as to advice or suggestion. Apparently the church would continue to pay the rent without question, though there were three, and would soon be four, wage-earners in the family.

When these facts were discovered, the church committee was asked to advance money enough to pay for the girl's lessons at a school where dress-cutting was taught, and to notify the widow that her rent would no longer be paid.

The girl accepted the offer at once. She proved a great success, and to-day is earning a salary as a designer equal to that of many college professors. She educated her younger brother in a profession, and has entirely forgotten the days when the church helped her. Her social affiliations are in another part of the city, and she bows, or forgets to bow, when she meets those who may remember it, as they would, to her credit. Had the church retained its claim on her through its financial aid, she would not be where she is to-day. Her development came when the church made another future possible to her by refusing to pauperize the family.

We all know the families who have more turkeys at Christmas than members. We still have churches and sewing schools in the same neighborhood, giving their Christmas entertainments at different hours and at different dates, to suit the convenience of those who attend both and profit thereby. We even have different entertainments given for different branches of work in the same church at different hours. We succeeded in impressing one boy with the idea that what he received at the various organizations maintained for his profit was "Christmas loot," and that he was clever at getting more than his share. We have become accustomed to conducting an exchange after our Christmas entertainments, because in giving we have, unfortunately, duplicated the gifts received elsewhere. Mollie finds herself with two dolls and no bed, and Katie has two beds and no doll, and Alice has two sets of dishes and no table. Like fate has attended the gifts to the boys. We, as a result, enact the rôle of patient, sweet generosity and redistribute gifts.

We know that comparisons are made as to which church, sewing school or club is the one to give the major portion of the coming year's attendance. But all this will disappear as rapidly as sectarianism and competition between churches and in philanthropic effort disappear. Competition created it; coöperation will dispel it, because all will come to a higher conception of the relations of efforts toward improvement. Then the "profit" of church and Sunday-school attendance will not be measured by the "things" distributed.

Nothing marks the growth of public intelligence more than the federations, and the systems that have grown out of the knowledge of the injury done the poor by misplaced generosity. Sometimes the children of the poor seem uncanny in the knowledge they possess of how to use the public and private charities.

A girl of seventeen gave astonishing evidence of this in a family crisis. She was a member of a working-girls' club; quiet, studious, reserved. She was always one of the poorest dressed girls in the club. Her devotion to those classes which she joined and attended regularly attracted the attention and admiration of the club directors. Discovering that her dress was in part responsible for the treatment accorded her by two or three members, it was decided to make it possible for her to make a better appearance. She had shown qualities which, if allowed free play, would make her an influential member of the club.

It was discovered that she attended a near-by mission of a Congregational church. Consultation with the mission workers brought the unwelcome knowledge that the mother was immoral, hopelessly immoral, but that her children loved her dearly and that she was devoted to them. The paying of rent seemed to support a shelter that ought not to exist, but no one had the courage to attempt to separate the mother and children.

Even this girl of seventeen had no idea of her mother's wrong-doing. It was a case that needed the wisdom of Solomon to solve. Just before Christmas the mother fell ill. The passion of grief that convulsed that group of children was convincing testimony of the mother's tenderness and devotion. Her eyes followed them constantly. When able to speak, she would whisper: "What will become of them? There is no one to care for them." She was removed to a hospital, with the knowledge that the rent had been paid for a month and that the children would be looked after. She died two days later. When the house was visited that morning, the elder girl was out "getting things," the children said. When she came in, she was told that provision had been made to send them all together to a home, where they would not be separated for a month. The girl sprang to her feet, grabbed the fifteen-months-old baby from the floor, and swept the others in a circle about her. She panted, rather than said: "You shall not take the baby away! I will not let them go! Nobody shall take them. They are mine. I can take care of them. You just pay the rent. I can do everything else. See?" She put the baby down, and thrusting her hands into her pockets, brought out tickets to the Diet Kitchen, the Charities Department for coal and groceries.

She had been to two missionaries connected with different churches she knew, and secured orders on a near-by grocery for dry groceries. There was not a public or private charity that gave outdoor assistance that that girl of seventeen did not know just what must be done to get their help. The amount of knowledge of this kind that she possessed was astounding.

Besides, there was not an institution in the city where children were taken for longer or shorter periods of time that she did not know. In many of them she had been herself. In others she had visited the other children of the family when they were inmates. She found out the defects of each one—the kind of matron, of food, of punishments that governed in each, and made out a case against each one. White, with blazing eyes, she looked capable of doing just what she said she would do, take care of the family of five little children. They were grouped about her, clinging to her, all crying in the face of the awful calamity that was about to befall them—separation. It was agreed that they should stay where they were for the balance of the month. The question of the future beyond that would be discussed later. The girl quieted down.

The mother had been insured in one of the insurance companies on the weekly payment plan.

The girl had secured an undertaker who would go to the hospital and take the mother's body to his establishment for the funeral to be held the next morning.

"We will have our own minister," she said, with dignity, "not the mission." Her visitors were again astounded. The mission had looked after the family for years. The girl had for several years been connected with the Sunday-school. The address of the minister was secured. The girl explained: "My mother was confirmed in that church, in her own country, her own home. She had a letter to the church when she came to this country with my father after they were married. At first my father earned good money, but he got sick and they did not get along, and my mother stopped going there, except to communion; and for three years now she ain't had the clothes to go even then. She had us confirmed there as soon as we were old enough, and we went there to communion when we had the clothes. The minister is going to come to the funeral, and I am going to send word to some of mother's friends from the old country who go there to church. I could not have them come here; mother would feel awful." Glancing about the barren, dirty rooms with a look of scorn, she continued: "We could not let our church friends know how poor we are. Mother tried hard enough. She was away from home days at a time looking for work. She took boarders. She did everything she could. You know I've worked when I could get it." Her voice broke for the first time. "She took boarders and gave them the beds; we all slept on the floor. She married the last boarder, the baby's father. She told me to stay here until he came home, this month—he's a sailor—and to do just what he says. He was always kind to me and gave me things. You've paid the rent, and you need not do anything more. I'll stay right here and keep the children till the baby's father comes home; you need not trouble any more."

She was quiet a moment, but evidently felt the doubt and the decision in her visitors' minds. Rising, she said fiercely: "I'll not; I'll never let these children be taken from me!"

The problem was too much for her visitors. They decided to leave the question of the immediate future to the family's own minister, who certainly had not carried these lambs in his arms, nor watched very closely over their erring mother.

The family was separated. Nothing else was possible. The baby's father repudiated any responsibility for any of the children, and disappeared. The girl drooped for a time after the separation; but she finally secured a good home, making a capable, devoted servant until she married. She owes allegiance only to her own church, saying: "The minister talked so beautifully at mother's funeral." Her whole conception of the mission church is that it is an institution for helping the poor.

She never doubted her mother, whose picture, enlarged from a small photograph, is the chief ornament in her parlor, her most cherished possession, outside of her husband and children.

In spite of the outburst of passionate devotion at the time of her mother's funeral, this woman, now with a comfortable home of her own, knows nothing of the children for whose protection she attained, for a time at least, sublime heroism. In a few months her indifference was as astonishing as her devotion had been. Her own life and its concerns filled her mental horizon to their entire exclusion. For her own home and children she has the passionate love that she gave to her mother and the crowd of half-brothers and sisters. She is ambitious for her children, and has two in the High School. This woman is a fair illustration of the evolution that is making this nation great.

The churches, when first the social disintegration began, had neither the intelligence born of experience nor the money to place the mission work in charge of people of high intellectual and social development. There were no training schools for Christian workers, and to that degree the Church was hampered in inaugurating its work among the poor. The selection was too often a question of pleasing some wealthy member of the church, by giving positions to protégés who had absolutely no qualification for the work but their necessities. This basis of selection—not yet wholly eliminated—put the work of the missions under the control of men and women who lacked social training. Neither by nature nor grace were they fitted for the work they attempted to do.

Their attitude of mind was too often that of patron, which, as any one of experience knows, is one of the most demoralizing influences active among the poor.

There comes to mind now a downtown church, the mission of one of the leading uptown churches. It was Thanksgiving evening. For weeks placards had been on the front of the building announcing an entertainment for that evening, to which all the people were invited. On the platform were a number of young men and women, sons and daughters of the uptown church members, the entertainers for the evening.

The church was packed with the people of the region, self-respecting poor. The mission, fortunately for them, was limited in money, so its possibility for pauperizing was limited to just that degree. The mission pastor, before the entertainment began, opened with a prayer, in which he thanked God for the warm-hearted, generous people who were giving themselves and their money for the uplifting of the poor and degraded. God was asked to implant a feeling of gratitude in the hearts of those assembled to enjoy this pure entertainment provided for their benefit. When he opened his eyes he continued his theme in two variations for twenty minutes longer, in what he called an address. It was this attitude of mind on the part of many of the workers that drove out of the church the mass of the poor; that began the breach that has widened, until in September, 1901, we stand appalled as we realize all that has entered into the making of that awful national tragedy.

The standards of cleanliness and beauty maintained in the mission churches have been far from what they should be. As the visitor enters to-day one of the first buildings erected on the East Side as a mission church, he is repelled by the general air of neglect; the dirt on walls and ceiling, made still more repellent by water stains from leaks; the ugliness of the whole interior, as well as the entire lack of adaptation to the work of to-day, which one of the most devoted of pastors, a friend to every man, woman and child in the region, is establishing. There is not one thing in that building that is not ugly and cheap. The very platform on which the pastor preaches lacks furniture, that would impart an air of cheer or impressiveness. Instead of the building being an unconscious influence in the neighborhood for beauty, tidiness, cleanliness, it is a part of the general result of the greed and poverty which has made one of the most sordid, character-destroying neighborhoods in New York.

One Sunday afternoon, as the writer was passing this building, the children began pouring out of it. The Sunday-school had just closed. They yelled, fought, ran. Suddenly they discovered a half-drunken wretch of a woman reeling down the street. The elder boys pulled her clothes, dragged off her hat, tormented her, yelling and laughing at the foul language they called forth. It was appalling, yet not surprising. The building remains as first erected. No attempt has been made to adapt it to the needs of the region. It was built for church and Sunday-school services, and the work which the devoted, consecrated pastor has put into it to meet the needs of the time is done under conditions that make the highest success impossible. There is not a room in the neighborhood for boys' clubs, for reading-room, for pleasure, where boy nature can have the fullest expression under wise direction. For adults the saloon and the streets are the only resources outside of their overcrowded homes. The pastor knows that to succeed in changing the character of that neighborhood it is necessary to hold the people through seven days of the week. He knows that this can be done if he can provide for the people pleasures, opportunities that express their social development. He knows that people express themselves in their pleasures, and that, whether they will or not, that expression is controlled by environment. If the trustees will not, cannot be made to see this, let the pastor of the mission be what he will, his work will be limited by the men who, in the very nature of their relations to the mission, cannot see the truth.

The pastor of the mission had a long vacation given him. The man sent to take his place wore soiled linen, would sit for an hour at a time tipped on the back legs of his chair. He would refer to the people in their presence as "they" and "these people." One of the young men who belonged to a club where some attention had been paid to manners and dress said one night: "Say, wouldn't you think that feller would wear clean collars, and stand up when talking to a lady? I don't care if he is a minister, he ain't much."

The people who were responsible for putting that man in that position were generous, held the best social positions, filled responsible positions in the commercial world. Not one of them would have chosen that man to represent them in the business world, because of his carelessness in dress and lack of manners. But they did not hesitate to send him to represent the Lord Jesus Christ to the poor; not a demoralized and degraded people, but a self-respecting body of Americans, born and trained, so far as they had been trained, to believe in the equality of man under the flag and before God. Is it any wonder that the more intelligent of the people resented the placing of this man over them, and remained away from the church of which he had charge? His person, his mind or his manners were not contradictory.

One evening, going through the audience room of this building on an errand to the rear room, the visitor heard one of the women missionaries say to a little girl who had evidently been troublesome and inattentive: "If you don't sit still, Mollie, I'll come there and shake you until you'll be glad to sit still." The woman was training a group of little girls to take part in a Christmas entertainment. They were each to recite a verse and turn a gold paper-covered letter as they recited, so that when the last one had spoken her verse the sentence "Glory to God in the highest, peace on earth and good-will to men" would be revealed. The woman, in temper, language, conception of her duty to these children, differed in nowise from their ignorant, tired, worried mothers at home, who probably made no claim as a teacher of morals and religion. What ideals of womanhood did this woman represent?

A minister came to attend the funeral of a little baby in a surplice so soiled and rumpled that a friend of the mother, who was a good laundress, said afterward: "I wish he'd given me that yesterday morning. I would have washed and ironed it." "He wouldn't have worn it if it had been a rich man's child," was the little mother's response. "Well, he acted like his surplice, rumpled," said the first speaker. And the writer was struck with the perfect characterization of the man's manner.

Fortunately, there are men who see the divine in every human being; who know that sorrow, grief, shame and suffering bear as cruelly, as bitterly on the poor as the rich, and in their ministration know no difference between them.

The writer was present at a funeral in an East Side home in a tenement having sixteen families.

A wife and mother had died. The family occupied the floor through. Nothing was known to the writer of the creed of the family, though she had known them for years. The minister came in a spotless surplice, most carefully put on. His manner of greeting the family and friends was so expressive of fraternal sympathy that one felt it a privilege to witness it. He stood in that East Side home the herald of hope. Since the blow had fallen he had visited it every day. On the day of the funeral he had so filled the hearts in that home with the spirit of resignation that the lesson that it taught left an impress on all who were present. Not once in the earnest address did he use the word "death." It was "release," and he made all feel that gratitude for relief from cruel suffering was the occasion for the assembling of the friends together. He gave out the hymn "Nearer, My God, to Thee." There was no musical instrument in the home. All present were wage-earners. The writer trembled for the result. The minister's beautiful tenor voice started the hymn, assisted at once by boys' voices in the different rooms. He had brought the choir of his church to assist, and stationed them through the rooms by direction before they came to the house. The people all sang. When the services were over, this minister remained with the family,

A SPIRITUAL BULWARK.

a courtesy which to the poor is so unusual that the memory of it is still one of the events of life on the East Side.

This represents this clergyman's attitude toward his people; and all who are their friends are his people. Is it any wonder that they never go beyond his care? He has baptized the children of three generations. Easter service is the homecoming of these families. They come from as far as they have money to pay their fare. The gray stone church is pretty. It has stained-glass windows, a baptistry, and maintains a surpliced choir. It is delightful to see the positive influence of these accessories on the people. Other churches to which they have access lack them, and the contrast deepens the love for the old church. It needs renovating, a parish house, a corps of modern workers. But these can well be dispensed with while that towering gray head leads the people. For the noble, unselfish life of the man stands before them always, the embodiment of eternal love and sympathy, interpreting both under conditions that would at times seem to justify doubt.

There is another phase of the Church's attitude toward its work in the poorer districts that lies at the root of the rejection of the Church by the majority of the thinking, self-respecting poor, and that is the assembling of the poor together as an exhibit of its work; the making of reports of which the poor are the statistics. The defence that this is necessary to stimulate the interest of the rich, and by that means secure the money for the continuing of the work in the poorer sections of the city, is but the evidence of the lack of spiritual life in the Church; the absence of the very foundation of Christianity and brotherly love.

The consciousness that watching the hungry eating Christmas and Thanksgiving dinners is hardly what Christ meant when he gave forth the decree, "Feed my lambs," is becoming a conviction; but it is due to the positive teaching of workers outside of the Church, who felt the irreparable loss of self-respect that must follow from such an exhibition. To gather the beneficiaries of their generosity together and take stock, as it were, of the investments, the dividends of which are to be realized wholly in the future life, has antagonized the self-respecting poor. They refuse to assemble as objects of interest, even in a church.

So dense is the spiritual perception of even some very good people, so materialistic is the plane on which work for the poor is conducted in some churches, that the results have been cruel—unconscious on the part of the offenders—but nevertheless cruel.

A group of very young girls worked in a factory on the borders of a section in which lived people of wealth and intelligence. The factory made no provision for a lunch room. When the weather permitted, the girls ate their lunches on the curbs and on the stoops of houses in the immediate neighborhood. This was demoralizing to the girls and distressing to several women in the neighborhood. Not far away was a large house hired and controlled by a church long noted for its broadness and its generosity. The basement of the house was not used, except twice a week in the evening by a working-girls' club. The use of this basement from half-past eleven till one was asked for and granted.

The plan was to have a woman arrange the tables, make tea, and wash the dishes used by the girls each day. The girls were to pay five cents a week for the use of the room and the tea. They were to bring their own lunches. The plan met with their warmest approval, and the lunch room was opened, with three young girls from a society in the church to help. The girls poured their own tea. For three days everything promised well. The girls accepted the one condition imposed, that they would go quietly to and from the factory at the noon hour, to avoid comments from the residents about. The fourth day some of the righteous, energetic souls belonging to the church thought they would see the result of their generous gift of the use of the room for which they had no other use.

Nine of them, personally conducted by one of the assistant ministers, crowded the two doorways to see these girls eat the lunch they brought from their own homes and drink the tea for which they were paying all they had been asked to pay. One small girl, with her hair still hanging in braids down her back, tried in every way to break off pieces of her luncheon without uncovering it. Finding she could not, she gave up, and tied the string about the paper again, sitting quietly with her hands in her lap. It was this child's first week out of school. Her father was now in the hospital for the third month. There were five children, of which this girl was the eldest. All the money saved by this skillful mechanic and his thrifty wife was gone, and this girl had to go to work. One can imagine faintly her feelings as she looked at the crowded doorways and knew that the whispered comments included her. The less refined, though more independent, girls sat with flaming cheeks, and holding papers over their lunches, ate them and drank the tea.

The first week represented the life of that lunch club. The girls went back to the curb and the sidewalk and stoops as lunch rooms. Here, at least, no personally conducted parties came to view them. If any one looked at them and they objected, they were on terms of equality, and at once notified the offenders of their offence. To the credit of the people who used that street, few stopped to look at the girls.

It would have surprised those very good people to have known the opinion those crude, uneducated girls had of them. A day or two later, standing with a group of girls who had not been present, with a half dozen of the men who worked in the factory, as spectators, the leader of the girls described the scene, caricaturing the "church gang," as she called them, and some of the girls who had been distressed by their presence. The group shrieked with laughter; yet there was an unpleasant note in it. "—— them! That's what they always do. Stay away from them after this," was the comment and advice of one of the men. "You bet!" responded the girl actor, as she curveted down toward the factory in response to the whistle calling them back to their work.

If the years as they passed did not clearly reveal that the Church that holds the poor is one over which men of the highest intellectual and social training are placed in charge, the mistakes of the present would be extenuated. Such churches do exist. Men of strong, vivid spiritual perception have erected and maintained bulwarks of righteousness in neighborhoods where the environment, the civic order is degrading. They have done this by conducting all the departments of their work with the view of developing the gifts of the people to whom they are ministering. The choir is the boys and girls trained by the best teachers they can secure. The Sunday-school teachers are the working boys, girls, men and women who are instructed by the pastor for their Sunday-school work. The officers of the church are the men of the neighborhood. The people are married and buried from the church; the children are baptized in it. The preaching is teaching that salvation is of time, as well as of eternity. The sins of the people are made visible. The pulpit holds the mirror up to nature. It is a pillar of cloud by day and of fire by night, leading them into the promised land, made so by their own civic honesty, their own personal character.

These men do not have to make reports; to bow before a board of trustees. They do not have to suppress or expand to meet the ideas of theorists. A few men give them the financial support they need, and let them, like men, stand before God and their own souls responsible for what they do for the people whom, when Christ was on earth, He chose for His friends—the poor.

WHERE THE PEOPLE SHARE.

CHAPTER V.

WORKING-GIRLS' CLUBS.

TWENTY-FIVE or thirty years ago in New York the question of the wisdom, if not the necessity, of moving the downtown churches uptown began to agitate the pastors and church leaders. The congregations, or part of the congregations, who had contributed most liberally to the support of the Church were beginning to move uptown, crowded out by business and the incoming foreign element which settles near the shipping and factory districts. The new-comers did not support the churches, especially the Protestant, not even by attendance. It was natural that the churches should follow their congregations. Some sold their buildings to the sects that came with the foreigners; some made a brave effort to maintain a church for the people; some became missions, distributing stations to the poor people who had settled in the now overcrowded houses that formerly were the homes of one family. The change in the downtown communities was so rapid that no one could understand how to deal with the new element. The Church had to spend years in learning how to adapt its methods to the needs of the new peoples who settled by hundreds where scores had been. Not only was this feature bewildering in itself, but the people spoke an unknown tongue, were foreign in thought and sentiment; were social, rather than religious.

The saloon far outstripped the Church in the ease with which it adapted itself to the new element. The Church encountered not merely the new people degraded, but an environment that in itself was a tremendous obstacle to decent living. The Church shortly discovered an entirely unlooked-for evil, insidious, demoralizing—the political corruption of voters. The Church to the smallest degree only in recent times has come into the larger conception of its function as a teacher of good citizenship, a link between the voter and the ballot-box, preaching the duty of the exercise of the franchise governed by conscience. It took the moral degradation of the city to rouse the churches to activity as redemptive civic powers.

The corrupting influence of corrupt politicians was evidenced in the conditions that developed in sections of the city left to their control. As the years went on and the men of conscience and intelligence became more absorbed in business and profession, more given to money-making, because of increasing social demands, the city became, in the minds not only of these politicians, but of the voters they trained, a mine to be worked for personal gain. Ignorance contributed to the rapid degeneracy of the people in the old home sections of New York.

The saloon became very early in the development of the tenement-house sections the only social center. The result was an increasing of the drink habit and the establishment of political headquarters in saloons. Often the politician in embryo was the saloon-keeper, often the bartender. The social side of life thirty years ago was not a subject for church consideration and study.

The Church ministering to a people having standards of social life established by the churches, the outgrowth of its teachings and creeds, can ignore questions that the Church ministering, or trying to minister, to a people poverty-stricken, overworked, living lives barren of any pleasures but those of the senses, in an environment that of itself would be a deteriorating influence, must meet and answer.

The Church downtown discovered it must work seven days in the week; that its office, its function was secular, as well as religious; that its Sunday work was but one-seventh of its work, and that the six-sevenths must minister to that one. The Church must go out into the highways and hedges, to use a misplaced metaphor for a city street, and win the people. This evolution of conception marks a spiritual Renaissance.

Industrial training was introduced by the churches, the natural result of discovering the ignorance of the women of household arts. Far more valuable than the skill imparted to the children gathered in these classes was the contact with the earnest, refined women and young girls who were the teachers in the now established mission churches. The revelation was mutual. If the tenement-house child gained new ideas of cleanliness, of order, of neatness, of dexterity, of manners, the uptown teacher also gained knowledge of which she stood quite as much in need. When a panting, shining-faced child came to sewing school half to three-quarters of an hour late because she scrubbed the halls and stairs of a three-story tenement house to help her mother, the housekeeper, who paid the whole or part of the rent for the family by this service, the uptown woman of leisure gained a new view of life and its responsibilities. When the mission worker who was giving time and strength and knowledge as the expression of her faith and conscience, found children scarcely more than babies working far beyond their strength in the service of their families, the uptown worker gained a new conception of sacrifice, of poverty, and, what was far more important, a new conception of the causes of ignorance. The uptown woman of leisure saw that often children were sacrificed to greed; forced to become wage-earners by parents anxious to increase their bank accounts.

As time went on, they saw that, whether poverty or greed was responsible for the sacrifice of the children, the protection of the children was the safeguard of the State, of the nation. There came from this, by the process of evolution, the factory laws for the protection of women and children; the compulsory school law. In these latter days this last has been made ridiculous by the failure of the municipality to provide school accommodations for the children of school age, especially the children under fourteen living in the overcrowded sections.

The church workers in the tenement-house sections were able to find means to meet some of the evils of oppression, of poverty, of ignorance. They had concrete facts to present to a semi-indifferent public; but when the social side of the people in the tenements became a problem, especially the social life of the young people, the remedies did not present themselves. The legislation proposed and executed was restrictive, not recreative. It was not the function of the State or the Church to provide social opportunities for uneducated, overworked young people.

The older girls in the Sunday-school classes presented not only all the problems of the little children, but the larger one of social opportunity. The homes were too small, too overcrowded to give social opportunity to the family. Besides, there was that saddest of all features too often found in the home of the working girls—the absence of all sense of personal responsibility on the part of parents for the social life of the children, girls and boys. The children in all but the exceptional home were free to choose friends, free to go and come as suited them. Home was a place in which to eat and to sleep; a place of shelter; a place often entered only when there was no place to go out of working hours.

The problem of providing social opportunity faced the downtown churches. In the very nature of things the social opportunities the Church could offer must be limited; must be of the nature that appealed to the more quiet, the phlegmatic, the element that presented the least factors in the social problem. The parish house, the church house did not exist. All the amusements offered the people must be in a building consecrated to religious life and service. It was a serious question how far the Church was justified in introducing the purely social.

It was natural that the young women brought into touch with the young working girls in the Sunday-school should apprehend the restrictions that life in a tenement imposed on a working girl. Everything in this life tended to make her gregarious. She was born into a house probably overcrowded before she came into it; she slept, ate, lived with crowds. The street, her only playground, was teeming with children like herself. When she worked, she rubbed elbows with the workers on each side of her. She went and came from her work one of a group. The working girl lived free, and pleasure she would have.

The girl of wealth and leisure working in the mission Sunday-school, by her own youth and natural inclinations, could appreciate this side of the working-girl's nature, and with the same clearness of vision see the limitations imposed on the Church in trying to meet the social needs of the people for whom it primarily existed.

Visiting the homes of their girl pupils, the Sunday-school teachers discovered the limitations of the homes. Between the homes as they existed and the churches as they must exist, the social center for the working girl must be created that would meet her social needs. The streets were the working-girl's reception-room, drawing-room, living-room, where she received her most intimate friends; where mutual entertainment was provided in ways that made no drafts on purse or inventiveness. Halls were open for dancing, where her presence was so desirable that she was admitted free or at half the price demanded of her brother. Excursion grounds with dancing platforms were then popular within the city limits. The immorality of the present temptations that make perilous the way of the working girl in 1901 were almost wholly unknown twenty years ago.

The work the earnest-hearted women interested in the working-girl's life faced was how to enlarge her social opportunities in connection with educational opportunities that would meet her peculiar need, and which she would accept. New methods of intercourse, new places of meeting must be found.

Every organization that has developed in these latter days for bettering the condition of the people has its root in the doctrines of the churches; workers and money come from the people who receive their impulse from the teachings of Christ. These organizations are as truly as the churches the expression of brotherly love; the positive declaration of the consciousness that no man liveth to himself.

To Miss Grace H. Dodge the women of this country owe a great debt. She, from the standpoint of a Church worker, devoted and faithful, saw that outside of the Church, but governed by all that the Church believed and taught, the natural outcome of both, a social center for working girls must be created. This center must be independent of any other organization. It must be at once a natural expression of the working-girls' standards. It must be flexible, as well as progressive, during every period of evolution in each group; it must keep in touch with the least progressive mentally, the most progressive socially.

A place must be created where recreation was possible; where classes to meet the educational wants of every member could be established. Above all, a place must be made where wealth and poverty, education and ignorance, could meet on the common level of mutual helpfulness.

A conference with a group of working girls but strengthened Miss Dodge's conviction that this social center would not only give to the working girls the social opportunity that New York lacked, but it would give to the woman of wealth and leisure the opportunity to meet the people whom she must know if she would use her time, her money, her education wisely in the interest of social development.

With Miss Dodge as president, the first working-girls' club was organized. It marked a new epoch. It made the opportunity that had never existed—the working of rich and poor to secure the same end. This country reaps the benefit of this first step in altruism based on the highest Christian and democratic doctrines.

The working-girls' club has from that time been a positive factor in the social development of working women, not only of New York, but the whole country. It has enabled the students of economics and sociology to get at facts that have revolutionized theories. The working-girls' club taught the working girls themselves the causes of their economic disadvantages.

Hardly was the first club formed when the practical results inseparable from this new combination of interests and sympathies met the approval of all interested in the problem of the working-girl's life. Everywhere clubs began to form. The idea has been adapted and adopted by the churches. Working-girls' clubs of all degrees of development, under many kinds of constitutions, managed and mismanaged, are to be found north, east, south and west.

The question of support was one of primary

importance. Miss Dodge had studied this side of the question thoroughly, and from the first it was decided that dues must be paid by the members. As new clubs were formed, this question of dues was met differently. Usually the wages of the majority of each group of girls forming a club decided the amount of dues, and naturally the dues varied in the clubs. In some clubs the dues were five cents per month; in others, five cents per week; in some the dues were twenty-five cents per month. Even this amount could not meet the expenses of a club conducted to elevate the standards of the members by the environment, as well as the social and educational opportunities provided. The financial managements of the clubs differ greatly, and always have. Strenuous effort has always been made in some clubs to make them self-supporting; they seem almost to live for that purpose. Entertainments, sub-letting of rooms, fairs, every means is resorted to to accomplish this end. Naturally the members of such clubs develop a good deal of business ability; sometimes at the expense of qualities that in a woman count for more in life.

The highest form of club life developed among working girls represents, to the working girl, her college. She realizes, as does the rich girl or boy who enters college, that what she pays does not, cannot, pay for what she receives. This conception of the financial side of the working-girls' club management controls in the clubs, with few exceptions, to-day.

The club must give every educational and social opportunity that will meet the needs of the members. As the college meets the demands of its students in the electives it offers, so must the working-girls' club. As the college student must meet the financial obligations he assumes when he enters college, so must the member of the working-girls' club keep her financial engagement. As the college makes it possible for the worthy student to complete his course of study after financial disaster makes it impossible for him to meet his financial obligations, so must the working girl who has contributed to the life of the club, or who has shown her desire to profit by what it offers, be kept in good and regular standing when financial disaster makes personal independence impossible. In short, the working-girls' clubs that are conducted on the broader lines, and with the most comprehensive knowledge of our social conditions, are in management and purpose a college for working girls. The idea of self-support may have been strained for a time, but it was an error in the right direction, and led to the truer conception which regulates the management of the best clubs to-day.

It was curious, is curious, the attitude of mind with which some girls approach the club idea. There comes to mind now the effort to form a second club in the rooms of a club of several years' standing. The need of the second club had grown out of the refusal of the girls who earned from five to nine dollars a week in various employments to associate with a number of girls working in a tobacco factory, and earning on an average three dollars and a half per week. The last-named were rough in speech and manner, and far from stylish in dress—the standard of the elder club. The introduction of the girls from the tobacco factory to the club was the result of the sentiment of one of the members of the club, a bright, wealthy, healthy girl, a great favorite with the other club girls. She had wanted for two years to work with girls less prosperous than the girls in the club of which she was a member.

A large tobacco factory not far from where the club met attracted her attention, and she invited the girls working there to join the club. Twenty-two came to the club-room. Mentally they were in a state of nature. This group of girls represented just what intermittent school attendance, uninterrupted freedom of the streets, from the time they could walk alone to the present time, might be expected to produce. They were strangers even to the degree of social opportunities the members of the club represented.

Their standards of manners and morals were what the neighborhood in which they grew up made them. Their homes were in one of the worse sections of the city, in which an institution wholly charitable pretending to do educational work had been, not what was intended, an elevating influence, but the reverse for the children of this section. When these girls went to school they alternated between this and the public school, so that it was impossible to compel their attendance at the public school through officers of the law. The neighborhood in which most of these girls had been born and grew up was a section as remote from the life of the city of which it was a part as though it were in another country. Through it ran a thoroughfare in which were stores that could supply every want. It was another political unit where one man ruled, whose approval meant work in the city department, in the street railroads, on the docks; even in the factories, of which there were many in the section. The streets were in a shocking condition, unpaved and dirty, and no one objected because no one cared.

The tenement houses were formerly the residences of the prosperous. These houses were badly kept, old and unsanitary. Liquor saloons were on two, and sometimes three, corners of the streets through the whole section. Beer-sodden women were so common a sight that the women who did not bear evidence of over-indulgence were remarkable. These girls had never known personal ownership, even in a bureau drawer; not so much as the right to one peg on which to hang their clothes to the exclusion of others. It is doubtful if they ever owned a change of underclothing that another child of the family could not claim.

Naturally, the girls took possession of the clubrooms. Quite as naturally the older members resented it. It was seen at once that an attempt to have the new girls elected as club members would be equivalent to ejection. They were tolerated, but not tolerable to the older members. At the end of four weeks the two sets of girls lined up on opposite sides of the room, utterly refusing to intermingle. This passive attitude changed to the aggressive, which approached open hostilities so closely as to make the danger line. When this point was reached it was decided to form the new girls into a club by themselves. The rooms were not used every evening by the club for which they were hired. Sub-letting would give more money for educational purposes.

As this attempt at club-making is one of the worst, and for that reason one of the failures, it would be well to describe it:

The directors hired rooms each fall, in September or October, until the first of May following. As one recalls this club, it presents one of the best evidences of the barrenness of the working-girl's life in New York. Every fall for years a few notes written to the leading girls, and a group of twenty or twenty-five working girls, would gather and start anew on this club life. This method of conducting a club made it seem useless to spend money in making the rooms attractive. They were usually on the second floor of a house occupied by two or more families; the halls dark and bare; the rooms rarely clean as to walls and ceiling, barren of ornament. The floors were bare, and not infrequently stood sadly in need of scrubbing. They were lighted by smoking kerosene lamps, which but added to their unattractiveness. Frequently the caretaker started the fires a few minutes before the time for the girls to appear. Yet the girls came and remained winter after winter.

The new girls accepted the same conditions, and assembled one stormy night to form their own club, with several additions to their number of their own selection, among the rest their forewoman. The leaders of the club realized that she might be an element of strength; she might be the source of infinite trouble. She had been young many years before, a fact of which she was wholly unconscious. She was dressed in what at the time was called laquer—a warm shade of tan—silk, trimmed with bead trimming; a lace collar, and a most remarkable hat completed the kind of a costume that always is discouraging to a true club worker.

Naturally the forewoman was the spokeswoman for the girls. It was useless to attempt to draw out a personal opinion from the girls, all of whom worked under her. Knowing the wages of the girls, it had been decided that five cents per month should be the dues, leaving the girls a margin from which they might pay for classes. The indignation of the forewoman at the suggestion of five cents a month dues would have been amusing if it had not revealed her utter blindness to the poverty of the girls. Being determined that no girl there should be kept out of her club by poverty, the suggestion was made to the forewoman that as her wages equalled the wages of any three of the girls, and as she chose to join a club where the others received such small wages, she might pay the same dues, and each month make a donation to the club to meet its current expenses. She could see the dues alone would not do that.

The forewoman, after a few minutes, consented to accept the condition. The worried look left the faces of the young girls, and they beamed on the gracious lady who consented to waive her own dignity in their behalf. Perhaps it is well to state here that the forewoman never made any donation, and that she would have been dropped from the club for non-payment of dues but for the knowledge that such a step would mean that she would make the girls leave the club. She was by them considered a good forewoman, kind, and ready to help a girl if a girl tried to earn more money. She had to be consulted in everything attempted for the girls. Fortunately she was so afraid of revealing her ignorance, which was dense outside of her work, that she always supported the workers directing the club affairs.

This woman was taken ill. The director of the club found that she boarded with a family consisting of a father, mother and three children, living in three rooms. She was found lying on a mattress on the floor, destitute of sheets or pillow-cases. She did not own a nightdress. The tan silk dress with the bead trimming hung on a nail over her head, surmounted by the gorgeous hat. She was

A CORNER IN AN OLD SECTION.

very ill and penniless; yet the poor about her were devoted to her and considered her most remarkable.

Several years ago both of the clubs referred to consolidated with another club whose directors kept the club-rooms open throughout the entire year. After the consolidation a house of three stories in a good neighborhood was rented, and devoted entirely to the use of the club. Only those who have watched the development of these girls could appreciate what the club has done for them. Cooking and sewing classes, lectures on city government, talks on books, on art and nature; the weekly contact with women of culture and refinement, who carry the conviction that club work is a pleasure, that service for others is a delight, has borne fruit, and the girls in turn give their service to those whom they may help—oftenest the members of their own club.

The evolution of character through the contact with others is, after all, the highest attainment of the working-girls' club movement. It brought the working girl into entirely new relations. Constantly she was forced to see the folly of placing emphasis on the wrong thing.

A nice-looking girl, very well dressed, joined a working-girls' club. Her face indicated character and intelligence. She was elected to office, but never re-elected, for she was ignorant—too ignorant to perform the smallest duties in club life. She came every week on the social evening, always the best-dressed girl in the club. As she grew more familiar she grew snobbish. She lived in a very poor neighborhood, where her clothes must have been even more out of place than in the club-room. She held a position which required special manual skill, and in her own field was an expert. Unfortunately, she obtained an influence over certain girls and headed a clique. Every week she became a greater problem. One night a rather rough, but frank and intelligent, girl was introduced as a candidate for membership by a member who worked in the same shop. The girl who was the club problem had been away two weeks working overtime, and did not come to the club until after the new girl had been elected a member. The amazement of both as they faced each other as members of the same club aroused questions as to their social and family background. All that appeared was that they were neighbors.

The first reception to mothers was given by the club about this time. When the night of the reception came, the "problem" came in a new dress having a jetted front. Her appearance amazed the members, and made it clear that the "prob-

OPPOSITE A CORNER IN AN OLD SECTION.

lem" must be solved or eliminated. The new member appeared with two mothers, both plainly dressed, one not warmly enough. This one was timid, reluctant to enter the room, and but for the urging of the new member and her mother she would have gone home. She refused to remove the shabby shawl she wore, and adjusted again and again the straw hat, on which a narrow black ribbon was pinned. The "problem" stood in front of the mantel, surrounded by an admiring crowd. The two mothers and the new member walked into the room. It was a dramatic moment. The new member, with an expression of deep scorn, said: "You forgot to ask your mother; we brought her." The "problem" grew white and then crimson. The girls fell back and gazed spellbound at the shabby, uncomfortable, timid mother. The scales fell from their eyes. The "problem," so far as influence in the club was concerned, ceased to be a problem. A girl who would sacrifice her mother's comfort, who used her simply to keep house for her, could not hold any position in a working-girls' club.

The story crept out. The "problem" felt the loss of prestige. Clothes had satisfied her ambition; she had through them enjoyed a sense of power. The experience of that evening doubtless opened her eyes to things in life to which she had been blind. Again and again she was seen during that evening reception to look at her mother searchingly. She seemed to see her in a new light, and by its reflection, herself. The mother was afraid of her and showed it. The daughter, it was evident, discovered that fear for the first time and sought to overcome it. It was determined to hold fast to the "problem" and help her solve herself. Great progress was made. Her dress no longer astonished; her mother came to the club receptions comfortably and suitably dressed. Out of consideration for her mother, she remained in the wretched tenement, because the mother and the house had grown old together; but the rooms were now furnished. The new member had supplanted the "problem" as an influence in the club. The "problem" became engaged, and the club lost her. The man was a storekeeper in a town not far from New York. The girl married and forgot to take her mother to her new home. The mother remained a club legacy for two years, when she died. The daughter sent the money to bury her, but did not come to the funeral. Her husband is successful, and she is a social power in the Church to-day; a devoted mother and wife, strange as it may seem.

The centering of experience, the revelations of character inevitable in a working-girls' club, are the largest factors in educating the members. As the years go on, emphasis is laid on the right things. Harmony results, because a sense of proportion is gained. Girls who have had the benefit of a public school education that enables them to fill positions that prove they have had such opportunities, often in the beginning of their club life will manifest a feeling of superiority over the girl who works with her hands. But eventually some experience will reveal to them the pettiness of their estimate, and a readjustment of values is made.

A girl, long a member of a club, had won the love and admiration of all connected with it. She earned wages far above the average of working girls, a fact well understood in the club. She was always an officer, and a dependable power in the management of the club. The girls were to give a play. No amount of urging won this girl's consent to take part in the play. A girl who had taken a part dropped out, and some one must take her place at once. Now the girls refused to take "no" for an answer, and the favorite went down in the basement with the others who were in the play. Each had her book to read her part, as a help to the girl pressed into the service. When it came her turn to read there was absolute silence. The girl sat white and trembling, trying to speak.

At last jerkingly the words came: "I cannot read. I never learned beyond the small words. I had to take care of the children when mother went to work, while my father was sick. I went to work as soon as I could and helped keep them in school. They all read and write. I cannot. Now you know why I did not say 'yes.'"

There was silence for the space of several minutes. No one could speak. Then the baby of the club, the one everybody petted, whose very naughtiness was attractive, ran around the table, threw her arms around the speaker's neck, saying: "You're worth all the rest of us put together. We'll never give the old play. We all hate it." This followed by a half dozen kisses placed wherever she could touch the crimson, tear-stained face of the girl through her hands.

Education had been put in its right place in the field of accomplishment. When the entertainment was given, the girl who could not read was made manager, because no one could do so well.

For more than twenty years the working-girls' club has been a power in thousands of lives. The process of character building through accretion and elimination has been going on. Through its influence the club method has been applied under every guise, but perhaps it is just to say that it has been at its best where its formation and management has been purely democratic and absolutely non-sectarian. In the nature of things, in affiliation with any organization, it must take its place as the fraction of a unit, and be in its management considered always as only a part of a whole to whose success it owes an allegiance.

Now the working-girls' clubs have their State organizations, even their national organization. The Pan-American Exposition brought working girls to the number of five hundred together in a convention to consider the questions vital to club life and management. Can any one doubt the effect of this journey into the world, the first that hundreds of these girls had ever made? Of the readjustment of ideas, the revelation of beauty, the new birth of values, because of the vision of a larger world lying beyond factory, workshop, office, school-room? For it has come to this: that the professional as well as the manual worker finds inspiration in the working-girls' club.

As the years went on, a new problem grew out of the working-girls' club movement. The members married, but they were not willing to lose the social affiliations of girlhood; they were unwilling often, reluctant always, to sever club relationship. On the other hand, the members felt that a married woman should remain home in the evening with her husband. Often the married member would come carrying her baby, for the club represented the mother's social relations. The next step was natural, the forming of a club of the married members to meet in the afternoon. The first working-girls' club, of which Miss Dodge is still president, formed, as the Domestic Circle, a club of married members.

The A. O. V. Matrons at the Cottage Settlement are the married members of the A. O. V. Club, formed when the matrons were little girls. Other working-girls' clubs have contributed to the membership of other married women's clubs.

Naturally, the subjects discussed in these clubs are those bearing on housekeeping and the training of children. The training received in the clubs enables the married members to conduct their business with dignity and dispatch. They are trained to club life, and have learned how to avoid unnecessary friction.

Some clubs plan a winter's work ahead. These programmes show a broadening of interest and sympathy, not only in the technical affairs, the home and the care of children, but the larger affairs outside of the home that makes its environment. It must be that the girls who have been club members make more companionable wives than the women who have not had their opportunities. The children are always present at the meetings of the mothers. Various devices and methods are employed to entertain and interest them. What the mothers' club means to the little ones was unconsciously revealed very recently in the statement of a young mother: "—— is always home from school five minutes earlier club day. She runs home to get ready."

The working-girls' club has in the process of its evolution become a family institution.

CHAPTER VI.

A SOCIAL EXPERIMENT.

THE Residents of the College Settlement learned in the first year of their work in Rivington Street to sympathize deeply with the married women, the mothers in the region.

Mothers, after nights spent in overcrowded, unventilated bedrooms caring for nursing babies, began getting breakfast at five o'clock in the morning. Husband and children of every age must be wakened for work or for school, often irritable because of the unhygienic conditions under which they had slept. Friction and quarreling is to be expected when there is one wash-basin for the use of the whole family; one sink for the morning bath of the family when there is running water in the rooms. Breakfast of bread and strong coffee, perhaps with the family waiting turns because only three sides of the table are available, as there is not room to pull the table out from the wall to make the four sides useful. Floor space costs in the tenements.

Friction, adjustment and hurry do not tend to develop a serene spirit in the house-mother whose office is purely executive. How much less in the house-mother whose hands must do all the work of the home? When the working and school-going members of the family are cared for and have gone their several ways, there is left to the house-mother almost always a baby and another child too young to go to school, to care for and amuse. In addition there is the round of work—washing, ironing, mending, making, cooking—all to be done under limitations of space and conveniences; often with the handicap of ignorance. Whatever the advantage of self-made money-makers, the self-made housekeeper, taught only by experience, not only pays dearly for her education, but is more than apt to be satisfied with her self-taught accomplishments, thus increasing her disadvantages in the use of time and money.

Even with a small family the house-mother with the usual round of work would not have many moments of leisure. When it is a large family, with all the disadvantages of the tenement-house home, the days are not long enough for the work to be done. It crowds the hours, and accumulates until often discouragement and nervous exhaustion follow. If the mother have a conscience, she wars with herself, battling against conditions that she feels but cannot understand nor overcome.

Three hundred and sixty-five days in the year

the Residents found these mothers who needed the change of pleasure that made no demands on purses. Even good wages did not permit these families money to buy pleasure and recreation. Mothers, good mothers, grew old before their time. They often grew careless of their personal appearance, and by this risked their influence in their homes, separation from their children, alert and often overconscious on the subject of dress.

Then there were semi-apathetic mothers because of discouragement; the mothers who drifted, never having an aim in life or an ideal; then the mothers who long ago ceased to make any struggle against environment, every year becoming more inert; the mothers, now grandmothers, who were remembered only in time of need by their children. The Residents saw the need of the mothers of all types. How could the apathetic be awakened, the discouraged stimulated, the overworked rested and cheered? Hundreds, thousands of mothers were losing the best things of life because for them the activities that increase interest and sympathies could not be brought into their lives. Their environment made social opportunities in their own homes impossible. Husband and children, through contact with life in shop, factory, store, street and school, enlarged their interest every day; while the wife and mother came to a mental standstill, often losing interest in everything outside of her home; often failing through lack of knowledge and discouragement in making that a place of rest and refreshing.

The Settlement was the bright spot in the lives of hundreds of young people and children. The mothers who could be stimulated must be reached and held in a center where pleasure would be the controlling element and education an incident. There were mothers who had lost all desire for social life. It was found difficult to arouse in them even a momentary interest in the thought of seeing new things, new people. The grind of life had blunted all social instincts. There were women who on the social side of their natures were dead; could not be roused by any thought outside of the routine of their lives. Interest enough to do for their families what required the least effort of mind and body was all that was left. The hope in these homes was the children. To them the Settlement must give inspiration and ideals; the home would never give either.

In the second year of the College Settlement's activity a persistent effort was made to reach the mothers, especially the mothers of the more alert and active boys and girls affiliated with the Settlement, in clubs and classes. These mothers came, but never the same group twice. The smallest obstacle would prevent the very women who most needed social opportunity from accepting it. When they needed help, they came to the Settlement; they were most cordial hostesses when the Residents called; delighted in the opportunities the Settlement made for their children; but the habit of staying indoors, out of touch with any life but that of the tenement-house halls, was a fixed habit most difficult to dislodge.

Some of the workers who were interested in this question were led to conclude that it was only the exceptional woman in the tenements who retained the capacity to plan her work to secure a specified hour or two of freedom in a whole week. The life imposed on the tenement-house mother does not make time an element in adjustment of her day, still less of her week. The breakfast over, the day unfolds itself, and the mother is free to meet it. Only in the exceptional home is life considered in its relation to the time of day. One thing was clear: that in the homes of the better paid wage-earners the mothers did not get their share of life's brightness. A College Settlement worker, enthusiastically supported by the Head Resident, determined to secure it for some of them. Failures would not discourage the worker, for every effort would be considered an experiment until success was attained. The club idea had proved successful for the children and young people; it had for mothers of larger opportunities elsewhere in the social world; it might for these mothers. At least, it could be tried.

Twenty-two calls were made on the mothers of children and young people then coming to the Settlement, asking them to the Settlement for a certain afternoon in the following week. All accepted the invitation; ten came. The women who responded were told of the plan to start a club to meet once a week. There would be music, a short talk and refreshments. The plan seemed to please all who were present, and it was agreed to meet the following week.

At once a problem was faced. Some of the mothers came without hats, wearing not overclean aprons, and apparently looking upon the movement as some new phase of almsgiving. Others were alert, well-dressed, comprehended that they must contribute their share in money and interest or the effort would die out. The children of these two types of mothers could not be distinguished by outward signs. American public school life and the very atmosphere of the street life had already begun its leveling-up process in dress and independence. How could these two types be brought into a common social relation, when they held nothing in common but the experience of living under the roof with many?

It was decided to let the law of natural selection operate freely. The club was an experiment, and it must not start with preconceived plans; its life must be one of evolution. The next week only the alert women appeared.

The club was formed, a president elected, and dues placed at ten cents per week. This the projectors tried to reduce, but the members insisted that they could and would pay it. That it would cost almost that to pay for the cake and coffee, and they could help somebody if there was any money over. The club was limited to ten members, and filled at the second meeting. It enlarged to fifteen the next year. In its fifth year it numbered forty-five.

The subject of the first formal talk, informally conducted, as its subject demanded, was: "How long after the hair is out of curling-papers is it becoming?" This, of course, gave the opportunity of laying stress on a wife's personal appearance; the necessity of being as attractive as possible to one's own husband and children. That was, is, the keynote of the club, its creed, its religion to-day, when mothers and married daughters are members. The time of meeting was two o'clock, that the mothers might be at home in time

THE WOMAN'S HOME IMPROVEMENT CLUB AT THE SETTLEMENT.

to get supper for their husbands and children. Babies came with their mothers, and children in school came to the Settlement instead of going home after school. Many of the little girls belonged to a sewing club that met the same afternoon at the Settlement. The club, named in the first month of its existence "The Woman's Home Improvement Club," celebrated its eleventh anniversary at the College Settlement, October, 1901.

As the first anniversary approached, the members suggested an evening meeting, that their husbands might come. The proposition received the most enthusiastic support from the Settlement Residents. Husbands, all the children who worked, and a friend of each member—if married, her husband—were included in the invitation. Dancing and music occupied the evening. What a revelation! Fathers dancing with their own daughters for the first time; mothers with their sons; daughters and sons spellbound at the sight of their mothers and fathers dancing together! It was evident that the club was a feature of the family life. The husbands and grown children knew what had been talked about, what had been done at the meetings. One husband, watching his wife dancing with their son, said: "I don't know how you've done it, but this club has made my wife young again; she's as young as when we were married." This wife and mother of nine children at the club one afternoon wished there were a hundred such clubs. " 'Tis a mistake to just stay shut up." She waited a minute, and then said: "I had not bought a hat for eighteen years until I joined this club; I did not need it; I never went anywhere; the children did all the errands."

This was the very type of mother the projectors of the club hoped to reach. The first evening reception proved such a success that it was decided to hold one evening reception each month for the family and friends of the members. Thanksgiving and Christmas receptions belonged to the children. Apples, nuts, gingerbread, cake and peanut brittle, with coffee, are the refreshments for Thanksgiving evening; new milk for the children. The games are Blind Man's Buff, Going to Jerusalem, with the Virginia Reel as an alternate, because the little children can dance it. "America" and "Home, Sweet Home," sung in chorus, close the evening. More than one family is now represented by three generations on these evenings. At the first evening reception a father and son of twenty years stood side by side. When the father began singing, the son stopped and looked at him in amazement. This changed to one of enjoyment, as he said between the verses:

"Dad, I didn't know you could sing." "I haven't in twenty years, I guess," was the reply. Both father and son had good voices. The son had made the discovery that he had a voice, at the Settlement, in his club. He edged closer to his father; there was a new bond of sympathy. The boy's Christmas present from his father, mother, brother and sisters was a mandolin, the first time a combination present had been given. It was quite natural that the next year a table for the new parlor should be the gift of the children to the parents.

An incident occurring in the third year after the club was organized is, perhaps, as perfect an illustration of the lack of social opportunity in a tenement-house home as can be given.

One of the most faithful and interested of the members was a woman about fifty-seven when she joined the club. She was slow to respond to the club idea; to the right of personal judgment outside her own affairs. Her responses to a question that involved an expression of opinion was usually: "It don't make no difference to me." After a time she grasped the idea that she was one of many, but had equal rights with all the members in deciding questions relating to the club, and she began assuming responsibilities; expressing her views. In the third year she came to the president, and with every evidence of wishing to disclose a secret, said: Next week Thursday is my birthday. I never had a birthday party in my life. I've always wanted one, but never had the room, and I never had the dishes. Do you believe I could have a birthday party here next week?"

"Yes, I'm sure you could."

"I can't do much; and I only have two friends besides the club that I want to have. I want to pay for all the coffee and cake, that I may feel that it's my party. Just my two daughters, and my two friends, and my grandchildren—four, that's all. I've been saving the money for a year."

One night early in the next week the bell rang. A working man stood at the door. He handed a five-dollar bill to one of the Residents, saying: "My wife, she's goin' to have a party here Thursday. I want you to give her a good time. She's been a good wife to me. Don't tell her; just spend it for her;" and the man disappeared in the darkness.

It was decided to order a birthday cake and light sixty candles.

The day came. Every member brought a remembrance. Radiantly, tearfully happy stood the hostess. She loved music, and a sweet, gracious woman whose music wins the most cultured sang song after song. Time for refreshments came. In the front parlor a club of little girls were sewing. It seemed a pity that they should not see the cake and the candles lighted. They were told that the doors would open, a lady was having her first birthday party, and it would be kind to wish her many returns of the day.

The cake was brought in with the sixty candles burning, and placed before the hostess, a gift from her husband. "I didn't know," the wife kept whispering under her breath as she stood beside it at the table. The doors rolled slowly backward, and twenty children breathed "Ah!" Then in a piping chorus, "Wish you many returns of the day." A moment the woman stood still. Then turning a shining face on all about, she moved toward the children, the tears falling fast. Raising her hands and face heavenward, she said solemnly: "O God, what have I done that you should be so good to me?" The volume of her life was opened.

A cake with a few shining candles, a few friends with their little offerings, and the wishes of a few children, and to one woman God had reached out of His high heaven and selected her as the special object of His care and love.

Not all of the five dollars had been used. The hostess was asked what she wanted done with it.

She was radiant. "I'll give a party to those children what said that sweet thing to me." Suggestions of other uses were cast aside. The children must have a party—ice cream and cake. When she found out that cake and ice cream would cost more than the money in hand, she announced: "I will wait to give it. In a month I save money to put to it." She made all her own arrangements, and proved a hostess of resource and tact.

She received her guests most cordially. Perhaps the most wildly exciting hours of her life were when, after much coaxing, she joined in the games of Drop the Handkerchief, Blind Man's Buff and Going to Jerusalem, the last game sending her crimson and panting into a chair in the corner, with the children crowding about her shrieking with laughter.

Time for refreshments found her anxious and watchful. The members of the club had fallen into the spirit of the day, and nobody was grown up.

An incident occurred during the serving of refreshments which showed the educational value of a story written for pleasure, not education; at the same time a very deep compliment to the book. "The Birds' Christmas Carol" was a favorite book in the club. It had been read twenty-seven times in one tenement house by eleven members of one family, and four times by one member, who said she would own a copy whenever she could spare the money. She wanted to read it when she felt cross. As there were not chairs enough for all at the party, some of the children sat on the floor. The little daughter of the mother who wanted to own "The Birds' Christmas Carol" sat on the floor in front of her mother. She did something while eating her ice cream of which her mother disapproved. With a quick glance at one of the workers who stood near her, the mother said: "If I had been as wise as Mrs. Ruggles, she would not have done that." Mrs. Ruggles was a thoroughly appreciated character. Her struggles to equip her children were perfectly understood, as were her ambitions for them. The hostess of the day was as disappointed as the youngest child when the lighting of the gas told that the day was done. She was the last to leave, saying: "I never was so happy in my life. It has been beautiful. All my life I wanted a birthday party. Now I have two;" and she turned a radiant face to say "Good-night" as she went down the stoop into the gathering darkness.

The weeks went by. The club had tickets to go to Glen Island, through the generosity of Mr. Starin. In August another member had a birthday, and confided the secret to the giver of the birthday party, saying, "I wanted to give a birthday party as you did. I never had one in my life; but I could not get money enough. I tried hard since yours." In September the elder member confided this conversation to the president of the club, saying, "Now we will give her a surprise. She shall have the party. I have talked with every member. But we will not each buy her a present; we put our money together and buy her a dress." The president doubted the wisdom of this, and suggested a dozen other gifts. "No, we give a dress. She does not have as nice a dress as other members. It is not right that one member of a club should not dress as good as every other member. Why not she take that dress? She know we love her, and we give her this because we want her to look as good as anybody; she is so pretty."

The dress was bought and given by the oldest member of the club, who in her speech announced her views on dress, and the need of one member looking as well-dressed as any other member; that if one could not have things, then the others must share with her; that was being a true member. The dress was received in the spirit in which it was given. When it was found that it could not be made by the receiver in time for the next reception because she had so much work, it was cut and made by five members of the club. The wisdom of putting money together to buy one present was learned, and from that time on the custom has been to make joint gifts when gifts are given. This is done in families, greatly reducing the valueless things that were formerly bought when only a little money, a few cents perhaps, could be spent by each one.

About the time this club was established the kindergarten had been added to the vocabulary of philanthropists. The kindergarten existed as part of the secular work of many of the churches, and individuals here and there supported kindergartens. It was generally conceded that the mothers of the children did not appreciate the work the kindergarten was doing for their children; that too often they felt that permitting them to go was conferring a favor on the kindergartners or those who had asked for their children's attendance. The Residents and workers at the Settlement did not believe that this was a healthy attitude of mind. They believed it was responsible for the irregular attendance of many of the children, as well as the lack of punctuality. There was no kindergarten in connection with the Settlement, nor room for one, but one was greatly needed. Much as it was needed, it must not come until the mothers wanted it and were willing to work for it.

Miss Brooks was then at the head of the Kindergarten Training School in connection with the Teachers' College. She was consulted. The result was that the members of the Woman's Home Improvement Club became on several afternoons members of a kindergarten. They used the materials, took part in the games directed by Miss Brooks and the members of her training class. The names of the material used, the things made, the stories, the games, the songs, became a part of the vocabulary of the mothers. Some of the material was bought and taken home to entertain the children. The natural result followed. "If only we could have a kindergarten for our children!"

It was suggested that if seventy children could be found near enough to the DeWitt Memorial, where a room for the kindergarten was available, that perhaps the kindergarten would be established there. Over one hundred calls were made by the nine members of this club, which resulted in securing the promised attendance of seventy children. The Lowell Kindergarten was then opened at the DeWitt Memorial by the New York Kindergarten Association as a result of this effort. The difficulties the mothers put in the way of good

THE KINDERGARTEN OF THE COLLEGE SETTLEMENT.

work in the kindergarten was explained to the members of the club, who agreed to call on mothers whose children did not come to the kindergarten in time, or were irregular in attendance. It was most interesting to watch the growth of public sentiment in favor of regular and punctual attendance, not only at the kindergarten, but at school. If the kindergarten child reported Johnny Jones, who was a neighbor's child, as absent, the elder brother or visitor after school was sent to find out if Johnny Jones were ill. It became a badge of good motherhood to have the child in the kindergarten on time. Before this, through talks by doctors and nurses, the relation between health and cleanliness had been discovered. Cleanliness was imposed on their own children, and exacted from other mothers of kindergarten children.

The influx of Hebrews, toward whom the members of this club had a deep race prejudice, drove them out of this neighborhood. Before seven years had passed but four of the members were residents of this district. But a change of residence did not change their belief in the value of the kindergarten. Wherever they have gone they have sought it for their young children, who have found always intelligent and sympathetic listeners in their mothers to all the events and incidents in their kindergarten world. One mother learned accompaniments to songs, and the children sing kindergarten songs at the club entertainments, even those in the grammar grade join.

As time went on, the conviction grew stronger that the real pressure of poverty or lack of money, among the self-respecting independent poor came not on the physical nature but the mental and emotional. The pressure was incessant. There never was a time when there was money to buy pleasure. Months, years went by without life offering the opportunity for enlarging the mental horizon of thousands of capable, receptive, devoted mothers. To the children the Church entertainments were opportunities; clubs and sewing schools were doing their share, but the mothers were only onlookers. There was no active part for them except in the world of work. The churches provided religious opportunity and social opportunity, regulated by the Church environment. Hundreds were not attracted, and often one sympathized with their rejection of this kind of social opportunity, tinged too frequently with patronage, and of necessity, narrow in its scope.

Early in the history of this club the love of music was so evident that it was decided that the members should hear "The Messiah." That would be the Christmas treat that year. The cost of the tickets was far beyond the means of the members, but friends made the purchase of the tickets for every member possible.

Two days before the giving of the Oratorio, Mr. and Mrs. Gerrit Smith came to the Settlement and gave a recital. Handel's picture was displayed, the story of his life told. The themes of the Oratorio were explained, and then sung by Mr. and Mrs. Smith. A new world was opened. The night for the Oratorio came. The journey so far uptown was into a land wholly unknown. Carnegie Hall was a revelation of another world. Its size and beauty, the audience, all a revelation. From the opening bar to the close of the Oratorio the club members listened entranced. It was the enlarging of the world revealed by Mr. and Mrs. Gerrit Smith. As the chorus "Unto us a child is born, Unto us a son is given," closed, every one of the mothers sat with shining face but moist eyes. A new message had come. One little mother, whose battle so bravely fought won reverence for her, leaned down and whispered: "I'm so glad I have sons; I'm so glad. I think I know now what it means." The echo came back for weeks, yes, for years. One member, in trying to tell her husband, said: "I saw while I was talking how impossible it was to make him understand, so I said: 'John, you'll never know till you get to Heaven what I heard and saw to-night.' "

The result justified the effort. It was seen that it was wise to have the best of everything for the members of the club in the way of entertainment. Musicians have given most generously of their time and talent. Speakers who are sought for in the highest intellectual world have been secured for the evening receptions, when the husbands and working children and friends were present. The result has been to develop just at the level where it was most needed standards that protect the home from enjoyments tinged with vulgarity, and even crudeness is now detected and accepted grudgingly or with apology.

The hard times of 1893-94 gave a new opportunity to test the value of such a club. The stories of suffering, of helplessness, made it seem wise to control money to be expended through the club members. They were brought into contact with families who never before were reduced to the point of asking charity. About four hundred dollars was expended under the direction of the members of this club. Work tickets were bought and given to men and women whose life history they knew, men and women they had known for years. When cases of strangers were brought to their notice, they investigated and advised as to the best way to give help. To prevent eviction, payment of rent was the first effort of the club members.

The education they received was invaluable. For the first time it was possible for them to help others in a large way; they saw that the number they could help depended on the wisdom shown in expending the money on which they could call. Their indignation knew no bounds when they found they had been deceived, as they were in half a dozen cases of families brought to their attention. One case caused a complete revolution in their theory that if people suffered it was because the world was hard with them, had not given them a chance. One woman, a widow, was brought to the attention of the club early in the winter. She had one child, and they had not had a fire in weeks; had no outside garments to go on the street, because they had pawned them for food. They had eaten nothing but bread and coffee for seven weeks. Now they were to be evicted from the one room they had occupied, because no rent had been paid for two months. The club had decided that paying back rents only benefited landlords; that, having so little money and so many demands, rent in advance was all they could pay. They voted to move the woman, then to find work for her. It was decided that she must learn to operate a sewing machine. The Charities' Organization Society made that possible. After two weeks' trial, it was found that the woman could not learn. Then the society gave her a chance to learn laundry work, and for two weeks more money to support the woman and child—cared for by one of the members in turn while the mother was away from home—was given. Again the report came that the woman would not learn. Then the members decided to teach her. This individual teaching, with what the society had done, seemed to make an impression. It was decided that the woman could iron.

When this stage was reached the fourteen-year-old daughter of one of the members passed on her way from work a laundry. At the door a sign hung, "Hands Wanted." The little girl went in and asked about wages. The man at the desk laughed at her. "It made me mad. I just looked at him," drawing herself up as she told the story. "I said: 'I do not want the work for myself, but for a woman *our* club is trying to help; she's poor, and a widow.' Then the man looked at me, and told me to tell the woman to come. I told him we'd all been teaching her." The use of the plural possessive thrilled the heart of the workers; the club was a family possession. The woman

MAKING A SELECTION.

was told to go to work the next morning. As the little girl was returning from work the next night, she stopped at the laundry to ask about the woman; to walk home with her, if she were going home. She was told the woman had not appeared. Before going to her own home, the child went to see why the woman had not gone to work. The woman had overslept. For three weeks that little girl got up earlier and went after that woman, delivering her at the laundry as though she were a package. It was decided that the sacrifice was too much; if the woman was not willing to keep the work by her own effort, she was not worth helping. An alarm clock was bought and given her, and she was taught how to wind it. She lost the place before the end of the first week because she could not get there on time.

The club found out that there were people it was impossible to help, do what the world would.

This little girl during this period of struggle with this woman was met one Sunday afternoon. She carried a doll to which she was devoted, and for which she made a cloak that Sunday morning. "Isn't she pretty?" she said, holding up the doll. "I often wish I could see her when I'm working." What a combination of child and woman! As the years have passed, this little girl has paid the penalty of shop life. She has grown hard, aggressive, self-assertive, untruthful. If only her environment could have been different, she would have made a magnificent woman. The world of struggle has been too much for her; it has strangled the spirit of helpfulness.

The lessons of that winter have been well learned. Every mother in the club wants a trade for her child; something learned that has in it wage-earning promise because the worker has special knowledge.

The time came when it was possible to turn the attention of these mothers to the administration of those city departments that make the environment of their homes. The streets naturally claimed first attention. They learned to take the numbers of the street sweepers who failed to do their work; to take the numbers of the carts improperly and carelessly filled, and report them at the club meeting. Leaking roofs, broken stairways, unlighted halls, contagious diseases were reported, and conditions in the stores and factories where their daughters worked.

The criminality of concealing dangers that threatened many to protect one was comprehended. The club motto became "A helping hand to all."

The club members felt that it was possible for

them to give special help to little children. In a thousand ways the women in the house of many families find the opportunity to help children; often through the children they helped the mothers. Sometimes through personal influence they secured the regular attendance of children at school; sometimes it meant calling in the aid of the Society for the Prevention of Cruelty to Children to secure the rights of children, to protect them from evils in their own homes.

One day a wealthy woman who had lost a little girl told the president of this club this incident, which, she said, changed the course of her life. For months she had shut out the world. God and man were cruel. Nothing interested her; life was empty. She sat by the window in her home one November afternoon. It was drizzling and blowing. A little girl without hat or coat stood shivering and crying against the church railing opposite. As she watched the child her mind reverted to the clothes she handled so constantly, because they had been worn by her child. She sent for the little stranger, and when she went on the street again she was warm, tidy and comfortable. Then came the thought, "God never meant a woman should be a mother just to one little girl. She must be a mother to every child who needs her." From that day this woman has given her life and service to children. The story was told to the club.

One of the members, after the meeting had adjourned and while the refreshments were being served, was overheard saying: "Why, certainly it would change everything if every woman would live in that way. Think how many times you could save children, how many times you could help them, if you were their mother just for the time they needed you—often only a few minutes."

Months after a member reported: "Well, I don't know what you'll all think when I tell you what I did last week. I've been bothered because such a nice-looking little girl came every morning about school time and went upstairs in the house opposite. She carried a lunch-box and books. I would see her with a baby at the window, and see her in the morning run on errands. At three o'clock she went away in the direction from which she came. That child is playing 'hookey.' That woman is to blame, I said to myself. One morning last week I saw the child go to the corner grocery. I went after her.

"'Where you live, little girl?' I asked. She grew red and hung her head, and tried to get out of the store. I stand in front of her. 'No, you must not be afraid of me. I have little girls. I love all little girls. Where is your mother? Child,

AT THE SETTLEMENT—A STORMY DAY.

you deceive her. She thinks you are in school, and you play "hookey."' The child ran out of the store, crying. I went right upstairs after her. I knock. The woman would not open the door. I knock louder, then she come. When she see me, she tried to close the door. I put my foot in the door and keep it open. I say, 'You are doing wrong. I belong to a club where every member is to be a mother to every child what needs her. If that little girl come here one more day, I follow her home and tell her mother. It be bad for you if any child come here so young as that child. It is against the law for such little children to work. That little girl is playing "hookey," and you make her. You do that any more, and I make a complaint against you to the Children's Society. Good-morning;' and I took out my foot, bowed and went downstairs. When I got home, that little girl is running down the street where she comes every morning. I never see her now, and that woman do her own errands and mind her own baby."

The members applauded. A child out of school is a child to be looked after. It has been concluded by the members of this club that they can do their best missionary work in the houses where they live, by keeping their rooms and their children in the best possible condition; that every home, every child so cared for, is the best possible sermon preached, the purpose of which is to make life better.

The League for Political Education, the Woman's Auxiliary of the Civil Service Reform Association, the City History Club have sent speakers to the club, some conducting courses of lectures. Even the Assembly District work undertaken by the League for Political Education was attempted by the club, but did not succeed. It could hardly be expecterd that it would.

During all those years the members had been trained to self-government. All questions are decided by the majority. There came a time when the majority voted to leave the College Settlement. It was deplored by the projectors, but accepted. After a few weeks a small house was taken a couple of blocks from the East River. The house had a large yard, and by expending a small amount of money was made very attractive. The attempt was made to have the members of the club do neighborhood work. A very short trial proved this was impracticable. Two things were revealed: That the mother of a working-man's family has neither strength nor time to give away; that the very conditions of tenement-house neighborhoods require trained, impersonal workers. The women who gave time to the club work in the neighborhood neglected their homes and families. The few members who tried to do neighborhood work in the house used every advantage the club-house offered, which they controlled, to curry favor, to revenge slights, real or fancied, to themselves or their children. The best mothers made no attempt to do any neighborhood work. The house became a social center, an educational center. But it was not a success until paid workers were put in charge of different departments, with a very few volunteer workers; and the most faithful of these were women of wealth.

It was hoped that uptown organizations would establish branches of their work in this house. Some did attempt it, but it failed for the reason that so many efforts to better the conditions of the tenement-house dwellers fail. Women lacking the right qualities volunteered, or the work was important when other things did not interfere. Clubs were established to which the organizers came when it was convenient. Again and again children connected with clubs waited until darkness came, but no "dear lady" whom they trusted appeared. In another case, numbers were the standard of success, and scores were crowded in where units should have been. All this forced the employment of paid workers, and centered the responsibility on one until the burden was too great to be borne.

Added to this, the principle of self-government had given a one-sided development to some of the members, and friction would develop when large questions were to be decided, an aggressive minority combating a conservative and less demonstrative majority.

The reform campaign of 1897 began. The picture of the candidate of the Citizens' Union hung in the window. The Citizens' Union used the house and yard for its lectures. When the campaign was ended, the friction developed to the unbearable point, and it seemed, in view of the dissension, best to disband the club. The club voted to keep together and return to the College Settlement, if the privilege could be secured. This was generously given, and the club unanimously voted to return, pledging the members to give all the aid possible to the Settlement work. Since 1898 the club has again been a part of the work at the Settlement.

For six years this club has had a country clubhouse—a large house, easy of access, in New Jersey, admirably adapted to the purposes of the club. The house is surrounded by lawns and an apple orchard. Two kitchens make it possible for two families to occupy the house at the same time.

The rent is paid and the house cleaned each spring. All other expenses, including car fares, are paid by the members of the club using the house. The plan is for each member to use half the house for two weeks. By a system of evolution and working of the law of natural selection, four families use the house at the same time. Mrs. A. invites Mrs. B. for the two weeks that she is entitled to half of the house; and Mrs. B., arranging her two weeks to follow Mrs. A., reciprocates by asking Mrs. A. to remain for her two weeks. Cooperative housekeeping has developed, as has the sharing in the care of the children. The barn, equipped for the children, has been an endless delight. Two members have in the past been debarred the use of the house. One because of the character of the men invited by the husband; one because of the language used to her children. Both were asked to resign from the club, or to make it inconvenient to use the club-house. One resigned. The average number of people using this club-house has been between four and five hundred each season. Sick children of neighbors have been taken up by the members and cared for during their whole vacation. On Sundays, friends, relatives and city neighbors are guests.

There has never been any supervision over the house, except that of the members. Each member leaves the part of the house she has used clean for the one coming after her. For several years the club paid part of two months' rent, raised through entertainments. One year the members made a donation of thirty dollars. Broken dishes are replaced, and the cost of repairing furniture broken is paid by the member using the furniture at the time. The large parlor is a club-room, and used by every member who goes up for a day. A closet is provided with dishes to be used when picnics are given by the members. The theory is that the grounds—four acres—can be used by the members at any time, but the families in the house must not be interfered with in any way.

The story of this club has been told at this length because it has proved what can be done in broadening the life of women of natural intelligence living under tenement-house conditions; how the family can have a common interest, to which each contributes, a center that can create social opportunity for the friends of every member and the members of every family.

This club has been able to do much to lighten the burdens in the time of financial crisis for people who could only have been helped through such a medium. It was the help of a friend always. For years it has been able to distribute Thanksgiving and Christmas dinners; but it grows more cautious every year, for it has made discoveries of the abuses of the Christmas dinner-giving. Through the children it has been possible to reach other children who needed Christmas cheer, but who would not take it from ever so kind-hearted a public.

The long years of working together has cemented friendships that are the inheritances of the children, and sons and daughters have intermarried. Baby after baby finds its godmother in the club.

There have been mortifying failures, but there have been positive successes in the eleven years. The club has proved conclusively that the working-men's wives can be determining factors in arousing and demanding better environment for their homes; that the wife and mother who keeps in touch with life commands greater influence in and outside her home, where all that she learns is used to make that home better; that she keeps her place in her family best when she makes herself the companion of her husband and children; when she, as far as she may, is herself the source of their social life, and contributes to their mental interests by sharing with them all the educational opportunity that life gives her.

CHAPTER VII.

WITHIN THE WALLS OF HOME.

ONE day a group of unusually intelligent wives of working men were driving through Central Park in a Park carriage. All were mothers, some of grown children, yet it was the first time that twelve of the twenty (all but two born in New York) had seen Central Park. Coming back on the east drive, the closed houses on Fifth Avenue attracted their attention. Various suggestions were made as to what use these houses could be put in the summer, when one woman, slight, delicate and extremely nervous, said: "I don't want anything in those houses but the room, just the room. I've never had all the room I want. I would have if I lived in them." After a moment she continued: "The reason we don't love each other as we should is because we don't have room; we crowd each other. All the time I lived in my father's home I was crowded. How we used to fight! Fight in the night, as well as the day, just because we did not have room. The beds were so crowded that one of the young ones had to sleep across the foot. The big ones would keep their

YARD DAY AT THE SETTLEMENT.

feet up while they were awake, but when they went to sleep they would stretch out and kick the one across the foot. When I was so little that I slept that way, I used to lie awake in terror expecting the kick, and how I scratched when it came! I know we would have loved each other much more if we could have had room to grow up in, as the children in those houses do. And my mother! She didn't have a room to herself when she had the sickness that killed her."

It was pathetic to hear the revelations of the little miseries of childhood due to lack of room in the home. "My mother used to drive us out of the house to get a chance to sweep it," said another mother of children. "I remember lots of times standing down at the hall door, shivering, waiting for her to get through. I would go into the neighbors' rooms, but often they had got rid of their own children for the reason my mother had of hers."

"I tell you what used to make me mad; it was to have to wait for the others to get through eating," said another. "When I hire a place I always look first to see if the kitchen is big enough to pull the table from the wall and sit about it. I don't think I ever had any hot dinner when I was little, and it used to make me mad. When I had three children I moved just to get a large kitchen;

it ain't near so nice a place, but the kitchen is big." There was not a woman there who did not have a grievance against her childhood because there was not room. One of them with crimson cheeks told how she remembered the sense of comfort that came to her after the death of an older sister because she had a bed to herself; she said it was a long time before she knew the cause, for she missed her sister's companionship, but she was more comfortable; she enjoyed having the five nails at the foot of the bed for her own clothes. The woman who spoke first interrupted: "I never in my life had even a hook in the wall that was my own until I was married. We were so near of a size we could wear each other's things, and we did. The one who was quickest got the best of that size. You never knew whose clothes you'd have to put on in the morning. I'll never have but this child. She likes me. She hates being pushed and crowded. She has a bed and bureau of her own. Never, never until my husband can pay more rent will we have another child." She paid the penalty of death for this determination.

As one thinks of the number of human beings with all their belongings crowded into the floor space of a tenement-house home, the marvel at the endurance grows greater. Think of its limitations of conveniences!

To those who know the limitations of a tenement-house home, the criticisms and suggestions that the superficially informed reformers make on and for the hygienic management of these homes are at once the source of amusement and indignation. When stress is laid on airing a bed every morning, and one in imagination sees the only windows in another room with a breakfast table between them, a room already overcrowded with things, the only room for the mother and baby during the process, one wonders what the speaker would do under the same circumstances. Then when the horrors of dust are revealed and the necessity of keeping the floors clean by frequent washing is made to be imperative, one sees the bed that just fits between the walls at the head and foot, with half of its own space free in front of it, and again comes the question, what would the expert do living under like circumstances? What is needed everywhere is scientific knowledge in conjunction with intimate knowledge of the evils inseparable from the small dark rooms of even the best tenements, and then we will have suggestions that the woman can use—can apply to her own family conditions—who must do the work for a family within this space.

In the best of the tenements it will be found that where the tenants can afford a parlor, access to it is across the kitchen, where all the work of the family must be done. It will be seen at once the disadvantage at which the house-mother is when friends who are not intimate call. Nothing stands between her and the outer world but the door into a public hallway. The bedrooms admit of a bed, and sometimes, but only in the exceptional bedroom, a bureau. This is usually found in the parlor, if there is one, and in it all the clothes that can be folded, all the little accessories belonging to the family; to this, however, all must have access. If there is a closet for clothes, or if the family can own and house a wardrobe, it is usually in this room, and the common convenience of the family. The bedrooms, dark, offer no space for a washstand. The kitchen is the common wash-room. The kitchens of the tenement houses built in these later years are a marvel of inconvenience. The dish closet is a few shelves up near the ceiling, the lower one of which can be reached by a woman five feet four standing on the soles of her feet; a chair is necessary to reach the other shelves. Beneath this space is the pot closet, or it may be the stationary tubs, the top of which provides table space for cooking conveniences.

THE CHILDREN'S HOUR AT THE COLLEGE SETTLEMENT.

There comes to mind now one of the best plans for a tenement having four families on each floor on the East Side. The stairways are lighted by a window on each landing opening on an air shaft, and on each floor is a lavatory with a large window. Each suite consists of four rooms. The parlor has two windows on the street; a kitchen window opening into the parlor, never raised if the family have social standards; and a window on a large air shaft, or space between the two houses, on which the bedroom windows, which are large, open. The rent for these four rooms is seventeen dollars per month, and they are on the fifth floor. The kitchens in this house have been described. The family have to sit at three sides of the table; there is no room to pull it from the wall; even then one side is uncomfortably near the stove. The only space except the parlor for a refrigerator is in the bedroom. As there are three young wage-earners supporting the home, who are social, who are encouraged by the widowed mother to have their friends in their own home, this is not to be tolerated. The refrigerator is in the bedroom. It was in that room when it was occupied for four years by a girl dying of tuberculosis. Is it any wonder that the fight against this disease is again being waged in that family? Yet it is above the average of its class in intelligence, as the apartments are above the average in the region.

The very elementary necessity of space and place for privacy in taking a bath is exceptional. For space, place and light are necessary. A very bright woman, perfectly familiar with the limitations of the tenement-house homes, once said to the writer: "The truth is they cannot be clean if they are decent." A cruel truth which was brought forcibly to the remembrance of the writer one winter afternoon in an East Side home, where a mother was trying to bring up a family to the best of her ability. When the caller went into the living-room of the family a tub stood at the side of the stove, in which was the youngest daughter, a girl about eight; a brother of ten and his boy friend of twelve or fourteen years were playing checkers on the other side of the room. The mother was ironing. There was no consciousness of embarrassment shown by the children. The mother was ashamed, not at the exposure, but at being found out in permitting such an exposure. She was a member of a club where the training of children was a constant theme. The necessity of physical cleanliness, its relation to health, she had grasped, and her children profited by it. The relation between privacy and morals she had not grasped. It was as though a veil had fallen from her eyes as she looked at her daughter of eight standing naked before the two boys. Whether such a thing ever occurred again the caller does not know; that the mother never forgave the caller for finding her out she does know. The family had three bedrooms, but none would permit the placing of a washstand in them. One was the passageway from front to rear, for the family occupied a floor, but could afford only one fire.

Privacy is almost impossible in the tenement-house home. One bedroom is usually the passageway to the next, if there are two, or both bedrooms are passageways from front to rear of the home, and must be used by all the family. Privacy is impossible in these rooms, and there are thousands of just such apartments. Children must grow up in them subject to the limitations, restrictions and exposures their walls compel. This division of space must fix standards of reserve, of privacy, of social life. No amount of love, not even of intelligence, can save the children from the evils such division of space imposes on family life. It deadens the sensibilities. The insidious effects of this is not always realized, even by the intelligent parents who accept them as inevitable.

One hardly knows whether to laugh or cry at the inconsistencies of the standards of those who go to Albany to secure the passage of bills for the betterment of the conditions of the working people. We have secured a law compelling separate closets for men and women in stores and factories, a righteous measure in the interest of morality. But the closets in the tenements must be used by men, women and children of several families. A neighborly courtesy is the loaning of the key, to save a neighbor a journey upstairs. Children run in from the street, several at a time, for it is the only place provided. This publicity and freedom is the crying evil of the tenements, the one from which tragedies come. The marvel is that so few follow; that in spite, seemingly in defiance, of it all, characters develop that are beautiful, harmonious, true.

Can one condemn the girl facing the worst that can befall her who under pressure that her appeal justifies, yes, makes necessary, confides that her relations with the man who is the father of the coming child began when each were little things six or eight years old? A relation that grew out of lack of privacy, the intimacy forced by tenement-house conditions. Both families have gone far beyond their social position at the time these two were children, but the blasting of innocency has left its burning scar on the girl, and she must bear it alone.

Perhaps it is this necessarily open living that gives the love-making in the tenement region a character peculiarly its own. When interest between the sexes is aroused, it is expressed so frankly and publicly. There are times when restraint would seem to improve manners; but among the working young men and women one is constantly reminded of Adam and Eve in the garden of Eden. How frankly and unconsciously they must have shown their interest in each other, and how unconsciously they must have revealed their interest in each other to all the other breathing creatures. Perhaps nothing about the love-making is more interesting than that numbers add to the enjoyment of both lovers. Nothing adds more to the happiness of a wage-earning girl than to have her "chum" deeply interested in and deeply interesting to a young man at the same time she is. It seems to be conceded that two couples can have so much more pleasure than one. The terms applied by these young people to each other will reveal their social level in the wage-earning world. If the term "steady" is used where the world of wealth and leisure would use *fiancé,* the under wage-earning world is reached. If "friend" is used, the social ladder covered by that word, used in that sense, has many rounds. Knowing many working girls who would use the term "friend" when referring to the man they had accepted as a future husband, or who would in time hold that relation, the writer was constantly impressed by the unconscious protection the girls threw about each other. One would rarely hear of plans made that did not include two beside the couple engaged, or willing to be. Sometimes two girls were to complete the party. It is evident that the more means the merrier time. In every group of girls there will be two or three who cause anxiety; two or three whose influence, unchecked, may lead to trouble. It is not easy to restrain the young people, for so often the offenses are so naturally the result of environment that to speak directly of them would be most unwise. The chances are that reference to them would put the speaker in the position of possessing knowledge of an undesirable kind; it would seem to suggest evil. Often it would be a moral shock to many working girls to have their actions criticised from the impression their freedom makes before the cause is understood.

A young girl joined a club for young people. From the first she caused anxiety. Her face was innocent and attractive, but her actions with young men were just the reverse. At last it became necessary to speak to her. It was evident

MUTUAL INTERESTS.

that she attributed the criticism to what she termed "fussiness." Not the least modification in her manner followed. At last, after many interviews, she was told that she would never be spoken to again. If she offended in the club-room once more, she would be given her hat. That would mean that she was not to again enter those rooms. She confided to her intimate friend that no one had ever told her that what she did was wrong. After this interview, a modification of her manner was noticed, not because she was convinced she was wrong, but because she thought it wise to heed. A group of young people were returning from a picnic. Just after the homeward journey had begun, it was seen that this young girl was sitting in the lap of a young man whom she had always known; as children they lived for years in the same tenement. Beside him sat the young girl whom he had invited to the club picnic. The club girl sat so unconscious of any infringement of manners, public or private, that a young man who had grown up under the same conditions was asked what he thought of the act. He started at once to tell the girl to stand up, but was restrained. Evidently he was shocked, and the act was wrong from his standpoint, the only standpoint fair to the girl. A seat was made for the girl elsewhere, who, for the first time, showed distress, or rather anxiety, because of her own acts. Nothing was said to her.

Occasion was made to speak to the young man who had kept his seat and let the girl sit in his lap. He was a working man, and his hands showed it. All his life of twenty-two years he had lived under tenement-house conditions.

"Frank, would you marry a girl who sat in a man's lap in a railroad train?" he was asked.

"No," he responded indignantly.

"Do you suppose you are the only man in the world who has that feeling? What right have you to let any girl cheapen herself so that the man who saw her with you, doing what you permitted, if you did not suggest and encourage, would not marry her?"

The man's face grew white. He had a sister of whom he was very fond and very proud.

"What would you do to the man who permitted your sister, when she was tired, to do what you permitted a girl to do to-night—a girl who has no brother to watch over her?"

The young man was six feet tall. He rose to his feet, and, raising his hands toward the starlit sky, he said:

"As true as there is a God above me, I will never while I live let any girl do what

I am not willing my own sister should do anywhere."

After a moment's quiet, the chaperon said:

"I shall never mention this to the girl. I hold you responsible. You are stronger mentally, morally and physically, and are wholly to blame." Whether he spoke to the girl or not, no one knows, but never again was it necessary to even mentally criticise that young girl's manners with young men. Not only did her manners change, but the expression of her face. One grew to love and trust her, and ask her help for other girls.

The chivalry of the working boys and young men is constantly seen, unconsciously revealed. Sometimes it is dangerous the degree in which it shows itself among the finest of the boys. A sick girl, unable to go out, will command attentions so special and direct that the fear of her misunderstanding, and suffering because she has not understood, will make those interested who know the danger unhappy; sympathy from any cause will make a great-hearted working boy place himself in a position where he may be easily misunderstood.

It is astonishing how long the spirit of childhood will live in working boys and girls, even under conditions that seem never to justify happiness and spontaneity!

One Sunday a group of working men and girls went nutting, being duly and properly chaperoned. Four of the young men climbed a big walnut tree. The girls, with some of the young men, were gathered at the foot, waiting for the shower of nuts. The chaperon sat on a stone fence a little way off. The wind began to blow, swaying the top branches. One of the young men having a good voice laid himself along a limb high from the ground, singing "Rock-a-bye, baby, on the tree top." The others took it up and the girls joined in. Over and over it was sung. Then the girls and boys on the ground joined hands outside the span of the tree and sang "Ring around a rosy." Every singing game of childhood was enthusiastically played. Every one of these young people were poor as the world counts wealth—every one over eighteen—all had worked from the first moment they could earn wages. Each one had suffered the wearing anxiety of no wages when the family needed what they could earn, and yet they sang—they felt like children. No amount of money at the time could have bought them this happiness.

The sun poured down a glory of yellow light on the trees that seemed to have caught its color dashed with red flames. Across the field came one of the girls slowly—a girl who never had manifested any enthusiasm, except for dancing; who never gave expression to any emotion of feeling. It was thought impossible to move her. As she came nearer, it was seen that she was deeply stirred; her face was expressive. Putting her head against the arm of the chaperon, she whispered, rather than spoke: "I did not know trees were any color but green before." The tears were chasing each other down her cheeks, while her mouth was wreathed with smiles. The girl was over twenty. Had she been born in a family that would use the privileges of the varisour Fresh-Air organizations, she would have known more of the country. It was this year that she first saw the stars over the trees, and the moon at the full in the sky when it had a horizon. Obedience to her was not easy, but to her brother she gave it willingly; he had been her nurse in babyhood, her friend and companion in childhood, and was now her protector. In every plan of these young people he considered his sister first. If she had an escort, he invited some other girl to go with him; if not, he took his sister. The girl never manifested any interest in young men beyond their ability to dance well. She would find a dozen reasons for not dancing if she found herself on the floor with an awkward dancer.

This group of twenty-two young men and women, all from homes that would bar the door to charity, even when suffering, were fairly representative of the social standard of the better part of the wage-earning world of New York. Among them was the independent girl, the one who had no desire to be sought in marriage; she saw the worries of her sisters married to men having small and uncertain wages; saw the wearing side of motherhood rather than its joys. She skillfully kept her young men friends as friends, changing from one to the other as soon as she saw the line of friendship being crossed. The girl who never won attention till she wooed it was among them; the girl who was treated discourteously or neglected was one of them. The girl who was sought for exhibition because she dressed well, yet who never roused any deeper feeling, was there, for some of the men were very observant, and had standards of style for the girls they escorted.

There was the young man who willfully played with a girl's feelings; the young man who openly exhibited the love he had awakened, but to which he did not respond; the girl whose adoration received indifferent treatment, yet who was never entirely cast aside by the man too selfish to marry. In that company there was one couple who were sentimental in their actions; they would sit and hold hands, if permitted, rather than dance. As

THE FOREST OF THE TENEMENTS.

soon as it was discovered that their actions were influencing others, they were given the choice to restrain the expression of their affection in public completely or resign. The lesson was effectual. When it was seen that one of the young men was very deeply interested in one of the young women, that she was only semi-conscious of his interest, yet enjoyed it, while not at all interested in him, just a few words, pointing out how unkind it was to permit his interest to develop and how unfair to let him spend money for her when she never meant to hold any relation but that of friend, changed her attitude toward him. She made the young man understand her position. More than that, she gave her lesson to the other girls, and escorts were changed frequently; groups arranged to go to the theater instead of couples. As one girl put it, "We don't want any nonsense." Yet several marriages have occurred among these members, the new homes making centers of social interest for the others. The babies are objects of deepest interest to all, and it is a lesson to see the ease and freedom with which even the young men will hold them. Much is said of the "little mothers," but the "little fathers" are as unselfish and devoted a part of the family life in the tenements as the little mothers. When a great, strong young man picks up a baby with the ease of a woman, is interested in its ills of the moment, one is grateful for the hours that, as a child, he spent as nurse; sees the beauty of strength and tenderness, and the humanizing effect of the maternal in the character of a boy whose character must be molded by the environment of a tenement-house region.

The rapidity with which a complete change of standard of manners can be attained amazed those who watched these young people. Outdoor life was possible to them only on Sunday. When first the trips on the railroad began, the noise, freedom, constant changing of seats mortified those who chaperoned the group. The journeys began in the spring. One Sunday evening in November, when returning from a nutting party, a group of young people entered the car laughing, pushing, slapping one another The young men and women who had been going to the country almost every Sunday for the summer looked in amazement at one another, and with very evident disapproval at the new group. Yet they had offended, if offense can be committed in perfect innocence, in just that way many times a few months before. It is this adaptability, this quickness of comprehension of the little things, that give the outward stamp, that make the American wage-earning young people so intensely interesting, so wonderful in social achievement.

These young people were all Americans, of Christian parentage, as the word means, not Hebrews. The young women worked in shops with girls of Hebrew parentage. There were deep race antagonisms, due to many causes, but principally to the willingness of the Hebrews to accept any wages and work anywhere and any number of hours. These American girls grew to have the deepest sympathy with the girls of Hebrew birth when they found that many Hebrew parents coerced, while all regulated, the marriage of their daughters. That parents would dare to assume such authority in so personal a matter as marriage aroused the most extravagant terms of condemnation. One listening could well believe the hopelessness of trying to make one of these girls marry against her will.

No greater contrast could be conceived than the entire independence of these girls in their social relations, which they did not view as a privilege but considered a right. Beyond the fact that some of them must be at home at ten or half-past, there was no law but their own will. This freedom is one of the most serious influences in the life of working girls in New York. Were it not for their common sense and the knowledge of life thrust on them when children, the effect would be most disastrous for the country. As it is, in certain ways young men and women retain the frankness of childhood in their intercourse. One realizes what perfect equality between the sexes is when mingling freely with them. Doubtless this comes from playing in the street together from earliest childhood, with no favors asked or conceded because one is a girl, and the impossibility of privacy. This last is the saddest fact in the life of tenement-house children.

At the lower rounds of the social ladder in the wage-earning world the mother and baby are inseparable, if the mother does not drink. Night and day the baby is cared for, often in hopeless ignorance, but cared for. Often everything else is neglected. When the baby sleeps, the mother is too tired to work, too indifferent. When awake, the baby insists on being held. One is frequently reminded of the story of the woman whose moan when her baby died was: "What excuse can I give John now?" Yet the day that baby is able to walk alone on the street the mother loosens her hold. The baby finds its freedom limited only by its ability to remain upright, and to return to its home for meals and at night. "Throw me the key and a piece of bread," is often the extent of its demands from the sidewalk. True, the mother knows every woman in the block will be, in an emergency, a mother. The child learns to care for itself; it makes less and less demands on the mother, who may even now have another baby compelling all her thought and time. Above this scale, where home-making assumes importance, the child remains longer under the mother's care; is watched when on the street by glances from the window; is sent to school, and some oversight maintained over its school life; but the wage-earning period means emancipation from oversight often even at this level. Hundreds of girls start out and find work for the first time without any evident responsibility on the part of even good mothers. No amount of familiarity with this exercise of freedom deadens the horror of it to the outsider. Women, mothers of attractive daughters, will not know the street on which the daughters work. After one of the most disastrous fires in New York, in which many working girls perished, four mothers notified the police the next day that their daughters had disappeared. It was the failure to trace the girls and the advertising of their disappearance that led, through companions who had escaped from the building, to the awful conclusion that these four had perished in the flames.

Sometimes it would be difficult for a mother to go to the place where the daughter finds employment; but here, as in everything else in life, that which is deemed the more important receives attention. Perhaps it is the habit of trust, or indifference, that governs mothers' activities.

A girl will make intimate friendships unhindered, unguided by mothers who act up to the measure of their comprehension of the duties of a mother. Girls are admitted to the homes who are unknown outside of the workshop; they work with the daughter; no other background is known. The mother knows that other mothers are accepting her daughters on the same basis of knowledge. For their young men friends there may be, but as frequently there will not be, any greater sense of responsibility than for the girl friends. In homes where the income would seem to demand a sense of social responsibility it is found wanting, and young people come and go unhindered. If there are two or more young wage-earners in the family, their conversation may bring knowledge of what they are doing, where they are going. But they also make compacts at concealments of disobedience where there are laws to be obeyed.

The world has been shocked by the tragedies of death and disgrace that came to the homes of

THE CHILDREN'S PLAYGROUND.

two young working girls within the past year. In each case the father and mother had gone to bed with the daughters out in the night, where they did not know; one a girl of eighteen, the other less. The "cadet" system would never exist were the parents of every girl alert to train and guard her the more closely because she was a working girl.

Until by some direct process the control of daughters and of sons is made desirable, and then natural in the wage-earners' homes, the problem of family life in the tenements will remain unsolved. It is a question sometimes whether, and sometimes it is very evident, that by the giving up of wages to the parents the freedom of the workers, even though but children, from obedience and parental oversight is purchased.

Those who know working girls know how high is the average of morality. Years will go by in intimate relations with the same group of girls and no tragedy will mar it; no echo of tragedy among their friends. The hardness with which even the suggestion of looseness is treated in any group of working girls is simply an expression of self-preservation. A group of sixty girls, earning the lowest wages and living under the worst conditions, were watched five years and one girl fell. As one goes over her history from birth, any other result would seem a miracle. A girl arrested gave the first name and address of one of the girls in this factory. The case was reported in the papers. By an unfortunate circumstance, the working girl living at that number was away from the factory two days at this time. When she learned of the connection that had been made because of the chance use of her Christian name and her address, she told a lie as to where she was at the time of that arrest. The other girls struck until she was discharged. The girl was innocent of everything but the lie; investigation proved this. The girls would not recede from their position; work had to be found for the girl elsewhere. She was publicly marked. They could not convince everybody of her innocence; lots of people believed the story, and they would not work with her; go back and forth with her.

A room was hired as a lunch-room for these girls. They brought their own lunches and paid a small amount of dues, which were used to pay for tea served daily. The projectors of this little enterprise were girls of wealth and social position; three were at the lunch-room every day. By representing themselves as friends of the projectors to the caretaker, two representatives of a "yellow journal" gained access to the room. One, a woman, engaged the caretaker in conversation for some time in the hall, getting all the information she could give her. The Sunday edition of that paper contained an illustration of the room filled with wretched-looking girls, while young women holding up trailing skirts were passing cups. The text was as far from the truth as the picture. The working girls absolutely refused to go to the lunch-room again. At last they agreed that if the paper would publish a true account—that they provided their own lunches and paid dues, and waited on themselves—they would go back. The paper refused. Two of those girls would never enter the rooms again.

The working girl has suffered quite as much at the hands of yellow journalism as the woman of wealth and social position. Not one of these girls went to school until she was fourteen; nor during any year since she began working had she earned on an average more than $3.50 per week. Yet they had social standards to maintain, and compelled recognition of them by those who opened opportunities to them.

The inspiring fact remains that the standard of home life in ethics, as in necessities, is raising. Without doubt much of this is due to the improvement in the class of readers used in our public schools. They are not perfect in the matter of selection, but they carry messages to the hearts, as well as the heads, of the children, few of whom would pass an examination on their contents. Even the primary grades introduce the children to the best thoughts of all time, and the crumbs, at least, are carried to the homes.

The girls who belong to the working-girls' club carry with them everywhere the influence that is molding their characters to a brighter type of American womanhood. The Settlements soon become centers of education through the social activities they make possible to the people. They surpass the clubs in this, that boys and girls, young men and women, each have in them the center that makes possible social occasions that are within their means and under rightful guides; together men and women are trained socially. The Settlements have been in existence long enough to have the children that were the first friends of the Residents now the fathers and mothers of children. The years of contact show results in the homes established, in the kind of care and the ambitions held for the children still babies. Wages have not greatly changed from those earned by the fathers of these new home-makers; but money represents different values. The kindergarten is the first thing demanded for their children, and the seeds sown in the minds of these young mothers bear fruit one hundred-fold because it is prepared.

The kindergarten mother clubs have also borne fruit in the homes where even the youngest child has gone beyond the kindergarten's age. These mothers learn for the first time the need of sympathy; of living with the children through every period of growth; of sharing and of making together a home. The result is, the homes gain in moral fiber and moral purpose. The schools and the homes are brought into close relation through these beginnings, and the child finds its interests a unit, and home the place where its whole good is of vital importance. The mother establishes the home often on the basis of contrast. "It shall not be what mine was; their lives shall not be what mine was when I was a child."

The churches, many of them, provide for the social life of their people; these social activities must be of a character that wins those who have the least to contend with in themselves, who find a pleasure and inspiration in religious life, which often is far more a matter of temperament than of spiritual development.

One sees the highest expression of spiritual development in lives apart from the Church as well as in the Church. This it is that develops a feeling of reverence for any movement having for its object the bettering of the social life of the people. One learns that every vulgarity that becomes obnoxious; every freedom that is brought within the bounds of restraint by new standards of education and refinement; every influence set in motion because of the spiritual perception of the answer to the question, "Am I my brother's keeper?" means spiritual life growing toward that of the Master of time, whose laws are but two for the guiding of men, "Love the Lord thy God," "Thy neighbor as thyself;" and these make neither cross nor steeple necessary, for they may be obeyed in the heart and guide the life wherever it is lived.

LIBRARY DAY AT THE COLLEGE SETTLEMENT.

CHAPTER VIII.

FINANCIAL RELATIONS IN FAMILIES.

THE women of education who attempted to make the conditions of working-men's families better, found their own education advanced, their values of essentials greatly modified in some respects, greatly enlarged in others. This was due to the bravery, the unselfishness, the contradictions of character forced on their attention through the natural, familiar intercourse made possible through neighborhood and club relations.

Probably the most astonishing experience in working-girls' club life is the revelation of the entire lack of self-consciousness on the part of working girls as to anything remarkable in their giving up wages not only week after week, but year after year, for the benefit of their families. The closer one gets to the poorest paid of the working girls, the more common is this unconscious unselfishness. In fact, the girl at this level who would attempt to hold or even to introduce a business relation in her family relation, would find herself an object of contempt, even when the personal habits of those who controlled the use of the money she earned were of such a character as to certainly mean waste of the money, perhaps worse.

However one's judgment may at times condemn this unselfishness and recognize in it a positive evil, one's heart is thrilled by the spirit of loyalty and devotion of which it is the evidence. Three sisters belonged to a working-girls' club. They were all employed in one establishment and earned good wages, yet they never had clothes that made them even comfortable. It was a mystery. They did not belong to the race which too frequently make thrift a vice, but were descendants of one the world counts thriftless. The months passed on. One of the sisters became indispensable to the club. She had the rarest tact, while straightforward and frank. When the second winter came, the pressure of life on these girls was very evident. How to relieve it, how even to approach the subject without appearing intrusive and meddlesome, was the wearing problem of the club directors. After the holidays the influence of one of the directors was asked by one of the sisters in behalf of a brother. Then the cause of the pressure was unconsciously revealed. There were five brothers and a father in the family.

The story unfolded. For years these three girls had supported the family; the six men had always been the victims of cruel "bosses." Worthy, industrious, anxious to work, looking for work all the time, they never succeeded in finding work under conditions that made it possible for them to continue. The years of self-sacrifice had not shaken the faith of these sisters in the smallest degree. "What would happen if your foreman would become arbitrary and cross?" was asked. The reply revealed the whole conception of woman's relation to life as they held it. "It's different with women; they have to bear things."

Another year passed without any change, except that the sisters grew old faster than they should. A quiet, determined effort was made to influence these girls to pay board to their mother instead of giving all their wages. They listened to the argument that as long as they continued their present system the brothers would not work steadily. The sisters listened, but the system did not change. Every penny was handed to the mother for disbursement.

One morning in the early spring, three years after these girls had joined the club, word came that the sister who had grown dear to the club directors, to every member of the club, was dead. She had dropped to the floor at her bench the day before, and died in the night. "Greater love hath no man than this, that a man lay down his life for his friends." The sacrifice was complete. Standing in the room of death with the six able-bodied men for whom this girl had given up her life, the sacrifice seemed barren, for its fruits had been garnered in her own character and had gone out of this life.

A year later the mother sent for one of the directors of the club to have her plead with the sisters remaining that they would give her their wages as formerly. "They only pay board now; they refuse to do anything for the poor boys. 'Twas a bad day when —— died. Shure, she gave me every cent. Not one did she keep back. Ever since she died, the girls just pay board, not a cent more. See how comfortable they are. They bought waterproofs, both of them, last week, and Jim has no overcoat. —— would have bought him an overcoat."

"Yes, doubtless she would. I remember the winter before she died she wore a spring jacket all winter, and that her shoes had been broken for weeks before she died." "Shure, I know." Tears fell from the woman's eyes, and her face bore every evidence of sorrow. "The boys could not get work that winter. God knows they tried. They had to have clothes, and —— was a good daughter. 'Twas a bad day for me when she died." The mother had not the slightest conception of the sacrifice her daughter had made—a sacrifice that had cost her her life. Her thought was for her sons; their comforts were to be secured through the daughters, who were a secondary consideration.

When her visitor protested against the sisters working to support the brothers in idleness, the mother was indignant. When she tried to show the woman that if the boys were forced by hunger and cold to go to work it would be their moral salvation, the mother insisted that they did try to get work, but that it was their "fate" to have unreasonable "bosses," who made it impossible for them to work under them.

"Do you think the girls always work under conditions that are easy?"

"No; but it is easier for a woman to stand a hard 'boss,'" was the mother's answer, without any expression of sympathy. Again she urged that the visitor use her influence with the two sisters for them to go back to their old method of giving the mother their wages. When the visitor refused, the amazement of the woman at her refusal was pathetic. When the visitor confessed that she was largely responsible for the change in the girls' use of their wages, the mother's indignation rose to the point of abuse. That her boys were robbed was the idea fastened in her mind.

That the club was the enemy of that home was the mother's conviction.

The mental attitude of this mother is by no means unusual. It is a common thing to find mothers who insist on controlling the wages of daughters who make no exactions in regard to the wages of sons. The effect is to lessen the self-respect of the girls and the sense of personal responsibility of the boys. In the family referred to the experiment of paying board to the mother was watched carefully. It was a success. The effect on the girls was positive. They developed a sense of personal responsibility; they grew more dignified and more reliable; above all, they developed self-respect. The fight was a hard one, but the moral victory was won. The brothers either found work under men who were fair, or they learned to endure control and discipline under a "boss," which was probably what they needed. The girls grew to have a care for their father's and mother's appearance and bought them clothes. Never as long as the mother lived did her feeling of her resentment against working-girls' clubs die out.

After her death, the father and brothers agreed to pay one of the sisters so much each week if she would stay home and keep the house. The sister did it, though it meant hours of loneliness, and, from her point of view, dependence. She had taken courses in cooking and sewing in the club; she had listened to talks on sanitation and hygiene; she had learned the value of money through the management of her own wages. She created for that family a far better home than it had ever known under the shiftless, thriftless management of an undisciplined mother.

The daughter was able to pay more rent from the money given to support the house, and the pride and self-respect of the family were greatly increased by the possession of a parlor, which was furnished on the installment plan out of the weekly sum paid to the sister. The home became a social center for the friends. The boys bring even their girl friends to their home, because it possesses more attractions than any other place to which they have access. A banjo lies on top of a piano—hired—and two of the boys take music lessons. In a family of seven wage-earners, even though the wages of each may be small, the combined income is large in proportion to the standards of outlay, and secures more than comfort, if rightly managed.

In this family a home maintained at a social level is of greater importance than clothes, and all work to keep it. Sacrifices are made to buy things for the home by every member of the family.

The sisters are to these brothers the finest type of women, and no girl whom they meet quite comes to their level. The sisters will never marry. The home, the father and brothers fill their cup of interest. There is still a latent suspicion that men are non-dependable, and they must be in a position to meet emergencies; the unjust "boss" may appear at any time, and they may be needed. Their brothers are a trust and must be guarded.

A visit was made to a home in which a girl of sixteen was dying of tuberculosis. The plaint of the mother, even in the presence of the girl, was, "She was such a good child. She always brought home her envelope unopened." To the visitor this was at the time incomprehensible, as the advantages of the envelope to her were twofold, that it could be opened as well as closed. The child had worked nearly three years, had been paid her wages in a sealed envelope, which she always gave to her mother as she received it. This is the measure of goodness for husband and child in thousands of working-men's homes. This mother was unconsciously brutal. Whether from lack of sensitiveness, or because of a life spent in fighting just homelessness and hunger, to the very last hour of her child's life her moan was, "What will I do without her wages?"

Not once did that little girl hear her mother give expression to any sense of personal loss for her companionship. The child herself became weighed down with the sense of responsibility, and resented the lack of strength because it added to her mother's burdens. This was her regret, the only thing she mentioned: "I wish I could have helped mother till the others grew up. I've cost such a lot being sick so long and not earning anything." That was her estimate of life at sixteen.

A son went wrong in that family, and as the time approached for his return home, the mother moved, lest he should be annoyed by questions and comments on his absence by neighbors. No power could be brought to bear on that mother to make her move that the daughter might sleep in a room having an outside window. One influence came within the range of her experience, the other was beyond her comprehension, and her daughter died in an absolutely dark, unventilated bedroom, in which she had slept eight years.

She was a dainty girl, in spite of the bad taste with which she dressed, this second victim. She floated, rather than walked, and her cheeks were like carnations. The girls in the club all liked her, and their young men friends at the receptions showed at once how attractive they found this girl. She was reticent as to her affairs, except in the question of work. When out of work, she did not hesitate to speak of it and ask to be remembered if any of the club members knew where she could get work. At last she came quietly one morning to the director and said the doctor told her she must stop working for three months. The expression in her eyes filled the listener with fear. In a voice that trembled, she said: "I am the only one working. Mother has a baby and cannot work, and—and"—her voice lowered and her eyes fell—"my father will not be home for three months from last Monday. He got into trouble. He would not if he had been sober," she added, in proud defence. Two months later the end was near, and the girl knew it. All that could be done under the conditions had been done. It was little, for an unreasonable, drunken mother had to be reckoned with all the time. She would stand railing against the girl for not going to work when the girl could not walk across the floor for lack of strength. The girl was under eighteen, and her mother was the controlling power in her life.

One of the young men who had been frequently a guest at the club receptions worked in an office near the girl's home. He passed one day as she sat by the window, and she saw him. "If he knew where I lived, he'd come in and see me," she said with a smile, full of friendship as the young man turned down the street. "I'll run after him. I know he would like to see you. He asked about you at the club last night." She clutched convulsively at her visitor's hand, saying: "Oh, don't! I wouldn't for the world have him see this place." She closed her eyes, after a searching glance about the room. Of course, the mother broke out in wailing about how hard she tried to do for the children and how ungrateful they were—ashamed of their home.

The girl gathered her strength and sat up, her eyes blazing with indignation. "Mamma, I'm dying. I'll not be here another week. There are three more girls; I don't want them to live through what I have." Slowly, solemnly, she continued: "You have not been good. Papa earned good wages, enough to keep us all comfortable; you know what you did with the money. He stopped giving it to you, and you got what you wanted on credit. You kept that up. You know what happened to him. I went to work. You know what you did with my money. I could not keep it from you even when I knew the little ones were hungry, for you beat me and took it, unless I had spent it for groceries and meat and coal before I came home pay-day. I heard what the doctor said, that I was dying because I have not had food and have to sleep in that hole, or holes like it." She pointed to the horrible bedroom. "I am dying. You are planning with the insurance money to have a big funeral. Have your own friends, but not one of the girls from the club or their friends, even when I am dead. I don't want them to come here. Promise me," she panted to her visitor, "that you will not let them come." The promise was given.

The mother was shrieking, whether from grief, or rage, or remorse the visitor could not determine. That night death came.

The girl was buried from the church she attended. When the club members were requested not to go to the house, there was scarcely concealed indignation. "Did she ever ask you to call on her when she was well?" There was no assent. "Have you any right to intrude there when she is silent? The church is open to all." No comment was made. At the church early in the morning the young men and women friends met. The mother could not even that morning hold herself in control. The girl's secret was out, and a great sympathy was added to the love her friends bore her. Her memory was an incense because of what her life must have been. Her unconscious unselfishness, her devotion to her little

A STREET ON THE EAST SIDE.

brothers and sisters, was revealed to them when they saw her mother. Good fathers and mothers found new expressions of affection for awhile at least, while the sharpness of contrast stood out between the dead girl's parents and their own, her life and theirs.

The girl who presents the most difficult problem in club life is the one whose social impulses are dominant. Noise, activity, excitement, seem inseparable from her presence. This type of girl arouses enthusiastic friends. She leads because she is daring; because she does not in any experience question results. One such girl had been studied for months. There was a superficial response to the efforts to win her regard, but the response was too transparent not to be understood. The girl would speak to any man who looked at her. One day she was playing "tag" with the other girls in front of the factory where she worked. A rag-picker pushing a cart made some remark as he passed. The girl, Molly, gave a spring and alighted on the man's shoulders like a cat. She clung there. He began to run, but he could not throw her off. She twined her fingers in his hair, made him turn back and carry her to the place where her shrieking, laughing companions stood. She sprang off. Still holding the man, she made him get down on his knees on the curb to the girls and apologize. Like a bird she flew to the place where he had dropped his push-cart, and, pumping the handle up and down to make the bells jingle, she brought it back to the man, still exhausted by his unwonted exertions, and with a mocking bow placed the handle of the cart in his hand. Then she stood up straight and ordered him to move on, adding: "If you ever show your nose around here again, you'll get more than you got this time." The man ran as if for his life.

Molly then turned and saw the friend whom she had promised she would be more quiet on the street. Her face crimsoned as she came toward her. "I could not help it. You don't know what he said. He won't never speak to another girl minding her own business as he spoke to us. I won't tell you what he said; it was too bad." The girl was about seventeen years old. She had cut off her hair, and it was bleached. She wore the gayest hats, which only served to emphasize the poverty and shabbiness of the rest of her clothes. One day she passed her friend's house without a jacket. She ran, holding her hands under her arms. Her jacket had been bought with money earned by working overtime, a result secured by the most persistent effort and argument.

Now the jacket was gone, and the slack season coming. As five o'clock approached, the girl's self-appointed guardian took her station at the window to watch for the girl on her way home. She came skipping along, slapping her arms to keep warm. She entered the house reluctantly in response to the call, "Where is your jacket, Molly?"

"I ain't cold. I ain't a bit cold."

"Where is your jacket?"

"Really and truly, I ain't cold. I'm thin, but I don't feel the cold as much as other girls. I ain't a mite cold."

It was impossible for the girl to stand still. She was shivering with cold, and her teeth, which were beautiful, were chattering. After a time the explanation was given.

There were five in family. The girl's mother, a stepfather about fifteen years younger than the mother, a brother one year younger than the girl, and a feeble-minded sister of fourteen. The girl was the only regular wage-earner in the family. The brother was a worthless fellow, who bore every evidence of degeneracy and rarely worked. The stepfather drank, and worked only occasionally. Molly earned six dollars a week, except in the slack seasons, two a year, when she earned about three dollars a week for four weeks each time. She began working when she was fourteen, and had never kept back one penny of her wages. Her mother had bought her new hats, but in all her life no other new garment except the jacket had ever been bought for her. She never asked any questions about the money, but she supposed the rent was paid. When she reached home the night before everything was on the sidewalk, and her feeble-minded sister was watching them. The jacket was the only thing owned on which money could be raised; it was pawned. "Molly, may I call on your mother?" A reluctant consent was given.

The home now was in a rear basement, the ceiling just above the level of the yard. The mother and husband occupied the bedroom; Molly and her sister slept on a narrow lounge covered with Brussels carpet, every spring broken. It was a series of humps. It was impossible to sit on it. In reply to a question, the mother acknowledged that no provision was made to make it more comfortable. The brother slept on the floor. The rooms were dirty and overcrowded. Food was of necessity poor, and because of the mother's indifference and ignorance, was poorer than it need have been.

This was what Molly received for six dollars a week. The moment the mother knew who the visitor was, she began abusing the girl. One special cause of offense was the keeping back of overtime money to buy a new jacket. She evidently imagined that she did not get all the girl's money every week. When it was pointed out to her that the new jacket had paid half a month's rent, she refused to be mollified, because the money paid for it would have paid the rent for a month and a half. Of course, this extra money would have gone like the regular wages if it had been given to the woman.

The walls were covered with pretty advertising cards and pictures cut from papers. Not a vulgar nor ugly picture was on the walls. "Who put up those pictures?" "Molly. Shure, that's all she's good for when she's home, a-cutting and putting up these things." This was one more charge against the girl. Evidently the girl gave her wages, and gave them willingly; but that ended her interest in her home and measured the mother's in her.

It was decided to move the family into one of the model tenements and furnish a room for the girl and her sister, paying the difference in rent for one year, to see what the result would be in health and morals in that family. When the proposition was made one evening to Molly, her face lighted and she emitted a sigh of perfect consent. But the light died out, and an expression of almost self-pity supplanted it.

"No, I must not let you do it. It would be lovely to have a room for Katie and me alone. I must not let you do it." She was silent for some minutes; then, with eyes cast down, she said in a quiet voice that indicated that persuasion was useless: "I know them houses. They're awful nice. I'd like to live in them. They're awful particular. They won't let no noisy people in. They make them move right out." Then slowly, with burning cheeks, she said in barely distinct tones: "Mamma is noisy sometimes, and when she's noisy she gets into fights with people. There ain't no use of moving in there; they'd not let us stay. Then, Billy"—the stepfather—"and I fight. I never speaks to him, excepts when he speaks ugly to Katie or mamma. He's drunk a lot now, most all the time, and then he's ugly to them. He ain't to me, 'cos he knows I'd break his head; but he is to them, and then I has to shut him up. I ain't spoke to him since he struck mamma, just after they was married."

"But your wages give him a home and food."

"Yes, I know it, but I can't help that, 'cos he's married to mamma and must be where she is." There was silence again, and then the girl continued: "Mamma didn't do it so much till she married him; she's worse now. I wish I was dead;" and the head of many shades was buried with the limp, "frowzled" feathers in the sofa cushion. "No, I can earn enough to keep them where they are. I must not move; but it would be lovely," she added with a sob.

A couple of weeks later she came in the evening. It was raining hard. After a moment's silence, she announced, with shining face: "We have the loveliest baby at our house, born last night week. I wanted to tell you before, but I had to do the work night and morning. He's lovely." She fussed at her pocket and brought out a pair of baby shoes of worsted. "I got them with some money I earned overtime. You say I ought to get what I want with that money." The eyes of the hostess followed the lines of Molly's dress to her feet. Her swollen, purple foot was seen through the broken upper of her shoe. Molly was looking with pride and love at the tiny shoes on her knee. "I named the baby Willie, and I'm his godmother," she added with pride, without the slightest conception of the relation between "Billy" and "Willie."

"Billy? Oh, he's drunk; been drunk a week. I ain't let him in yet; I'm goin' to wait until the baby's bigger and mamma's up. She'll let him in," she added, with disgust.

Matters grew worse with the advent of the new baby, for Molly had to fight with her mother to get it cared for. At last it died, to Molly's pathetic grief. The mother had consented to Katie's removal to an institution, where she could receive care and training. Molly was persuaded she owed a duty to herself. No impression was made until her mother had been arrested twice. Then Molly consented to leave home. It was deemed best that she should contribute part of the rent to insure her mother a home and to maintain a natural human tie. Molly did this *for three years*. Then she married a man controlling a good business. Molly is a quiet, devoted wife. She married a man old enough to be her father. When the wisdom of this was questioned, she said, with emphasis and a nod of her curly head: "No young man for me, thank you. Look at Billy!"

It was Friday morning—a warm, sultry morning in August. The bell rang. A mother in black and a young daughter of eighteen were in the reception-room. The daughter had evidently been crying. "I've come to tell yer that Annie can't go to the country to-morrow. She's sick'm. She's cried all night. Her brother was discharged'm. He do be havin' a bad man for a 'boss.' He's discharged'm, and Annie can't go to the country with the girls to-morrow. I can't

A COOKING CLASS OF MOTHERS AND CHILDREN.

spare her wages. It's all I got. Shure, if I could get work in washin', or anything to do, I'd do it, but I can't'm. I'll look all the week; and the boy'll get somethin', perhaps. She can't go this week; will yer let her go next? Shure, the rent is due, and her wages is all I got for three of us. Yer can go to work to-day, even if it be a bit late, and yer can go next week to the country."

"Oh, mamma! the girls talk nothing but country. I can't go to-day," was the sobbing response.

The girl did not go that summer. There was no room for her until September. By that time the work at the factory had increased and not one girl could be spared. Patiently Annie commented: "It wouldn't be any good if they could spare me. My brother is out of work yet. He's awfully unlucky."

The quiet heroism of thousands of working girls can be appreciated only by those who become familiar with their lives in the natural intercourse of club life. There is, of course, the other type of girl—the girl who insists on spending the major portion, if not all, of her wages for clothes; who assumes no responsibility for the family, and who has conceded to her the right to spend her money for clothes. She would make life most uncomfortable if she were compelled to share what she earned, even when the family live under conditions that make the home merely a place of shelter—conditions that make even decency impossible. The fathers and mothers seemingly have no rights that this type of girl feels she is bound to respect. When such girls marry, the mothers will do the washing for their daughters, hold the menial relation, and neither mother nor daughter questions the justice of the relation. Sometimes the daughter will pay the mother for doing the washing, "to," as she expresses it, "help her mother out." Such families usually cannot be helped through any influence but the evolution that comes through environment and neighborhood development. There is a superficial difference in the social development of such parents and children. The parents concede the higher position to their children, and the children take it as a matter of right.

The wages of skilled workmen enable them to keep their children in school until they are sixteen or seventeen years old, if the children will stay. These fathers can support their families, but not dress them as they desire. The girls go to work for the sole purpose of dressing better than their fathers could dress them. This indulgence creates false standards, and is a serious blot on the American working-man's life. It prevents marriage. Both young men and young women understand that the wages of one cannot buy luxuries for two that the wages used for one bought. The army of clerks on small salaries increase yearly. This class, through association, develop tastes and standards of living that make impossible the establishment of homes on their incomes and at the same time the continued indulgence of developed tastes. No type of family develops less that adds to the wealth and attainment of the country than this type. The children are selfish; they marry; they discover that the wages that bought clothes to suit the extravagance of one is wholly inadequate to support a family. Discouragement, friction, ennui follow, and life becomes a grind, without hope, without inspiration. The second family slips backward, and it is but two generations from shirt sleeves to shirt sleeves, with this difference, that the arms covered by the shirt sleeves of the third generation lack the muscles of the first, as the spirit lacks its moral fiber. It is this type of family that keeps alive the most vexing of social problems. The skilled working-man's family, the family of the small salaried men, present the most difficult problems not only in the use of money, but the use of time. Their daughters are often far more helpless than the daughters of men of wealth. During their school days, except in the exceptional home, they are not trained to do housework; do not learn to sew. As soon as school days end, office or store work begins, and then there is no time to learn the household arts. If in these homes the money-saving value of time were taught, independence and freedom impossible in wage-earning would be secured; the standards of life would be the essentials, not the non-essentials, that so often rob life of what is best and most valuable.

Hundreds of girls become wage-earners because they dislike housework. Anything else is preferable. Dean Gill, of Barnard College, New York, in an address recently delivered, said there were three types of college girl: The girl who never could learn any of the arts of home-making. She advised that that girl be allowed to choose a career, and that men make no attempt to interfere with it. The girl who had in her the latent qualities that, if developed, would make her a home-maker. Such a girl it might be wise to keep home for one year between Sophomore and Junior year. And the third girl had the home-making gifts so well developed naturally that no amount of college training would modify them. This classification holds good of the daughters of men earning small salaries, wages, and no wages.

As the Domestic Science department is developed in our public schools, the homes of working men of the better class will benefit by it. This distaste of housework will disappear, because it will have gained a place equal in value to geography and mental arithmetic, and these will have value because a knowledge of them adds to the home-maker's ability.

There are homes of thrift and order where all must be wage-earners; homes where the claims of parents on the wages of children are conceded. There is a bank account, but on this the children have no claim, no matter how much of their wages may have gone into it, or how much educational opportunity they may have lost because its demands have been paramount. When the children marry they establish homes without any or very little help from their parents. They do not expect it. Home, food, clothes have been given them; all claims have been met. They are as free as their parents when they began. Usually there is a gift of a piece of furniture or table linen; but money to start a new bank account is not expected. Without doubt, much of the inability to use money to prepare for future emergencies is due to the fact that financially the new home-makers from these homes are infants in practical experience. The marvel is that they keep homes as well as they do, and meet the future as well as they do without planning to meet it.

The second generation of this type of thrifty families rarely carry the habits of thrift of their parents into their home-making. The new financial freedom is a novelty, and presents in itself enjoyment that the new home-makers use. Here and there is a recovery from the danger of extravagance by a young couple, but the recovery is rarely so complete as to repeat the restrictions that the thrift of the parents compelled in their homes. The new generation demand better clothes and better furniture. Food and rent are regulated to meet these demands.

One stands appalled sometimes at the degree of vitality, the hope and the cheerfulness that prevail in the homes protected only by the muscles of one man; what they can buy representing all that the home may have. There is no spirit of recklessness; there is no failure to comprehend the slight protection a husband and father can give, though he be skillful; but there is a sublime confidence in the future. Though familiar with suffering, if not personally, then sympathetically, with full knowledge of what sickness and death bring to other unprotected homes, such men and women, and there are thousands, live from youth to and through age cheerfully, happily, without any financial safeguard except against Potter's Field. This weekly insurance is kept up; the

A MEETING OF NEIGHBORS.

family live cheerfully, gayly, sometimes to the end.

One result of doling out small sums to young wage-earners, whether thrift or necessity is responsible, is disastrous, especially disastrous for young girls. It has seemed to the writer that if mothers and fathers could be brought to a realizing sense of its dangers, they would endure hunger rather than have their daughters exposed to it. After all, it could be averted by making a division of the money spent for dress. Girls are often dressed out of all proportion to the sums they earn, if a fair division of their wages were made, if the dignity of the daughters was protected by any degree of independence financially. Of course this disproportionate use of money is due to false standards that will only be regulated when the people on salaries learn to universally live true to the law of proportion in their expenditures.

It seems to be a fixed idea that a girl is dependent on invitations from young men for her social pleasures. If she is not invited, it is not only her misfortune, but her fault; she should be more attractive. On the other hand, the young man is scarcely any better off than the young girl financially, yet he expects, and his world expects, that he shall bear, not only his own social expenses, but those of at least one girl. His impulse is to be chivalrous, for chivalry is not regulated by income nor deadened by pennilessness.

It is oppressive at times to see how the lack of money prevents the natural association of young men and women; how often the young men are forced to give up the society of girls for this reason. Girls often unconsciously force invitations. As one goes down the scale, the girls invite themselves, where the young men have to bear the expenses. So small a matter as carfare will make a girl thrust herself on a young man's care. The girl will not resent indifference, even discourtesy and neglect, if only her aim is accomplished. The young men suffer the reflex of this attitude of mind, and their estimate of women is regulated by these misconceptions, and even their manner as husbands is regulated by this conception of the relations of the sexes, and wife and daughters suffer in consequence.

The higher up one goes in the social scale, the less evident is this aggressiveness on the part of girls, and the more natural relation of man as the suitor is apparent. As girls are brought more familiarly under the guidance of women willing to discuss the financial relations that should be maintained between the unmarried of both sexes, the more careful girls become in permitting the expending of money by men for their social pleasures; especially so where the limitation of a man's resources is understood, or even suspected.

How to make mothers put their daughters in an independent position where their pleasures are concerned is a very important and at the same time a very difficult question. When it is a question, as it often is, of the very necessities of life for a family and the allowing of money for the pleasure of a fun-loving daughter, necessities bear down the scale, even of justice, and dignity ceases to have value. For it must be remembered that the girl's wages, used for her exclusively, would often allow the exercise of independence in her social affiliations. This it is that makes Settlements so important in our social life. Here boys and girls do meet on a platform of independence, chaperoned naturally by those who know intimately the home surroundings, the social standards, the limitations of life in the regions, and all that creates environment, that most positive factor in the making of character. The social attitude of the young people who grow up in affiliation with the Settlements is found to differ greatly from that of young people untrammeled by oversight or influence that develops dignity.

The influence of working-girls' clubs is positive in its effect on the majority of the members. The girls are taught in the clubs directly and indirectly. It is not only in the teaching of the home arts, but through lectures, talks, books and contact with women of education. The members often astonish those who know them best by their responses to their opportunities. This mental development makes them critical. The men they meet rarely have had their opportunities, and they suffer by comparison. The young women often find they have larger interests and sympathies; far clearer ideas of the responsibilities of life; are better equipped than the men they meet. Every girls' club shows members who thus develop. Often they will not marry. They are the support of one or both parents, now too old to work; they help married sisters and brothers; they are the prop and stay of all the halt and lame of their families; wiser and better guides for growing nephews and nieces than their own mothers and fathers. Frequently they are the most important helpers in club life, exerting a positive, upbuilding influence. Yet one always grows sad when thinking of them. Not thriftlessness, but unselfishness, may leave them penniless in old age. There is no place for them. Rarely is there a corner to which they are welcome in the tenement house; often even where there is love and gratitude there may not be space.

THE READING ROOM AT THE SETTLEMENT.

Floor space often regulates the expression of love, where the heart may have unlimited space.

The saddest figure in tenement-house life is the unmarried woman who can no longer work and is dependent. In her effort to serve her people she may have played the critic, and that is remembered when her service is forgotten. It is this type of girl who by instinct refuses to accept attentions that mean the spending of money by men who cannot afford it. Their wages would, if used for themselves, have given social opportunities that did not involve obligations, but family demands seemed to make such use impossible. Sometimes the fun-loving sister will secure both shares. One is taken to a home of her own; the other left to carry the family burden, and no one questions why. If it is unanswered, it is attributed to the lack of attraction in the unmarried sister.

There are homes in the tenements where the wages of the earners make a family income, in which all share equally, independent of the amount contributed. There is a bank account. It may be in the joint name of father and mother, but it is far more commonly the unquestioned property of the mother. The children look upon this as the protection of the parents from dependence in old age, should it not be called upon by illness or misfortune. Such families represent the highest moral development in tenement-house life. The children have been trained to appreciate educational opportunities, and school is through childhood an important factor in life. When the wage-earning period comes, night-school advantages are appreciated and used. When the work is chosen, some thought is given to the promise of future wage-earning powers by the acquiring of skill in that employment. The maximum wages possible at the present time is not the controlling element in the decision. The future is not sacrificed to the present. Such a home is kept, no matter how small, in a condition that makes social life in it possible.

Hallways, street corners, store steps are not the only places for the development of the social instincts of the members of such families. After marriage the family is united, and home, though it be in the top of a tenement, is the Mecca for children and grandchildren.

At the other end of the social scale in this world of workers is the happy-go-lucky family. Here the system of financial management has its faults, but much is found that is better than wisdom in money matters. Spending extravagantly when there is money, going without cheerfully when there is none. Why, the going without is scarcely treated even with the respect of making it a subject of conversation. The habit of sharing when any member has anything to share becomes a fixed habit, and "mine" and "thine" are not in the family vocabulary. The result is a close and interdependent family relation, of which the mother is the center. Often you will find that this mother has never had any clothes that would do to wear on the street, except to early Mass, if she is a Romanist, or that she rarely goes to church, if a Protestant, because her clothes are not what she calls "fit." Her life is the gospel of unselfishness, and she reaps the reward of love. One may fret at the waste, resent the short-sightedness, which means ignorance and shiftlessness; but there is so much pleasure in these families, so much that means happiness in them, that one even learns to forget the frets. They never grow beyond childhood in worldly wisdom, and childhood is always attractive. It is so rich in promise. Happiness is the cement of human life. Poverty does not change its power of holding the members together through weal or woe. There is a common inheritance of memories that never lose their power of cohesion where love and friendship reign in families.

The people who do not know the lives of the working people can have no idea of the extent to which the working men trust their wives. The majority of working-men's wives are financially in a far more independent position than the wives even of capitalists, where the wives are without an independent income. Not only is the money given to the wives, but their use of the money is unquestioned. There is a constant revelation of the unselfishness of these men. Children will be overdressed, while the father will not even be comfortable; but there is no complaint, for the pride of the father is gratified. He, with the mother, has one standard—clothes. There are men who say frankly that they would waste the money if it were in their care; that their wives secure far better results than they could; that the practice of having only carfare, at the most lunch money, reduces greatly the much abused social habit of "treating." The married man who can "treat," it is generally conceded, is not fair to his family; he keeps his wages at their expense.

Sometimes the observer marvels at the infinite patience of many men. Their wives drift. Neither money nor time is used for their families. A week's loss of work, and there is debt; a day's sickness, and to its suffering is added the knowledge that there is no money in reserve to meet this emergency, even though the wages insure it. While knowing well the cause, one resents the un-

AFTER SCHOOL AT THE COLLEGE SETTLEMENT.

just conditions that control many marriages among the young people of the wage-earning class. The young women rarely have the knowledge that will enable them to do their share in establishing the home. The young man contracting a marriage without the prospect of supporting a home is condemned and his bride pitied; but there is little criticism if she spends years—years that mean discomfort and waste—in learning to do her part, if she ever learns.

The mental attitude of the wage-earners toward their income is confusing and yet interesting. In reply to any question of wages, the maximum sum is always given. The question of idle time does not enter into computations of the year's possible income and necessary outlays. This holds good before as well as after marriage. Work may last for only forty weeks of the year, but the other twelve, even among intelligent wage-earners, sometimes are not counted in their relation to income. This perhaps explains much that is counted as thriftlessness. It is, in fact, a failure to apply arithmetic to daily life.

After all is said, no one who is familiar with the income of the wage-earning class can fail to see that the results obtained prove conclusively that the use of money in the well-regulated home is a fine art; that many working-men's wives could give post-graduate courses in the use of money to women who consider they have the right to teach them. Even waste and misuse are regulated by education and experience where there is even a modicum of intelligence. The second conclusion is that thrift under certain conditions is a vice that causes distinct deterioration of character. It should be combated as vigorously as thriftlessness. It can only be done by raising the standards of living; by creating other standards of value than money.

But everywhere among the wage-earning people the independence of the wife in money matters is apparent.

There are men who are niggardly and who hand out small sums daily, and never recognize that the wife has a right to anything beyond food and shelter, who grudgingly buy clothes when they must. These men are despised, spoken of with contempt as not being good fathers or husbands, and their wives are openly pitied. But the mass of working men place their wives in a perfectly independent position by making them the absolute disbursers of their incomes. The small shopkeepers, to all intents and purposes, treat their wives as partners. The wives work with them, sharing their knowledge, their responsibilities, and appear as joint owner in the bank account. The wife usually is the safe until the money goes to the bank account.

When a wife is a good financial manager, she is the head of the house, whose reign is never questioned. "Her children rise up and call her blessed; her husband also, and he praiseth her," though the Book of Proverbs may be unknown. This financial independence of the wives of working men develops the spirit of independence and aggressiveness that so often disturbs and upsets the plans of the woman who would do them good, and is the cause of the charge of ingratitude that is often made against the women of the tenement-house regions. It is scarcely natural to develop gratitude for efforts made in the wrong direction. Poverty has its degrees, as has wealth. There are families living in tenements whose conditions represent wealth when contrasted with that of their neighbors. One fact remains. Both women do not need the same opportunities, the same help. The student of the management of wages in a tenement-house home rapidly acquires a spirit of humility. While everywhere there is waste, there are times when money seems to buy double the amount that the student thought possible. With the wage-earners' families, as with all others, the income buys that which is most desired by those spending it. Choice is the master of decision, even in necessities. What is needed in the wage-earner's family is that education, that opportunity for development that will make a choice of the highest things, those that will mean a body and mind so nourished and cared for that moral resistance is the available capital of every member of the family in time of need.

CHAPTER IX.

HOME STANDARDS.

THE world knows two aspects of involuntary poverty: The one inseparable from degradation; the other picturesque, appealing to the emotions, and giving a field for the play of sympathetic activity that frequently neglects to note the results it attains.

There are few who discern that poverty is a comparative term, and these do not use the word in its financial sense wholly.

Those who know intimately the struggling, up-growing poor know that the rich can never give the exquisite expression to love that life at this level makes possible. Who would dream when looking at the Hercules, with clothes and hands soiled by his daily labor, that he is the tender nurse of wife and baby; that he is hurrying to a house cared for with joy. He will wash dishes, cook, scrub the floor, walk the baby to sleep, and coddle and pet a wife who from sheer loneliness and worry over work undone may be the harder to please and quiet. All this, and perhaps, almost certainly, not once will any terms of endearment be heard, and, strange as it may seem, no kiss given. How one rebels and rejoices that love can be thus expressed!

When sickness enters the home of the poor man, money is not present to relieve the able from personal service, often made more difficult through ignorance. Pride shuts the door to charity and the burden is carried in love. Those who know life at this level can never, never lose faith in the Eternal love, for they see always, however disguised, the divine spark in every human being. The silence of love thus expressed, the revelation of it where least expected, makes the one who witnesses it conscious of what power lies outside and beyond and above his own life, not witnessed to the ear. Every day at this level of life in our great city it is proved to the privileged that tenderness is the winning element in strength; that love daily, hourly here proves its power of self-abnegation. Here, too, it fills its function of inspiration. Days, weeks, months, years go by and the burden of moral weakness is borne with the cloak of faith wrapped about its fears. When so expressed, its loyal unconsciousness adds to its beauty and makes it an inspiration to all who come into its presence as friends; the lips voice its faith, the eyes alone reveal its fears even to friends.

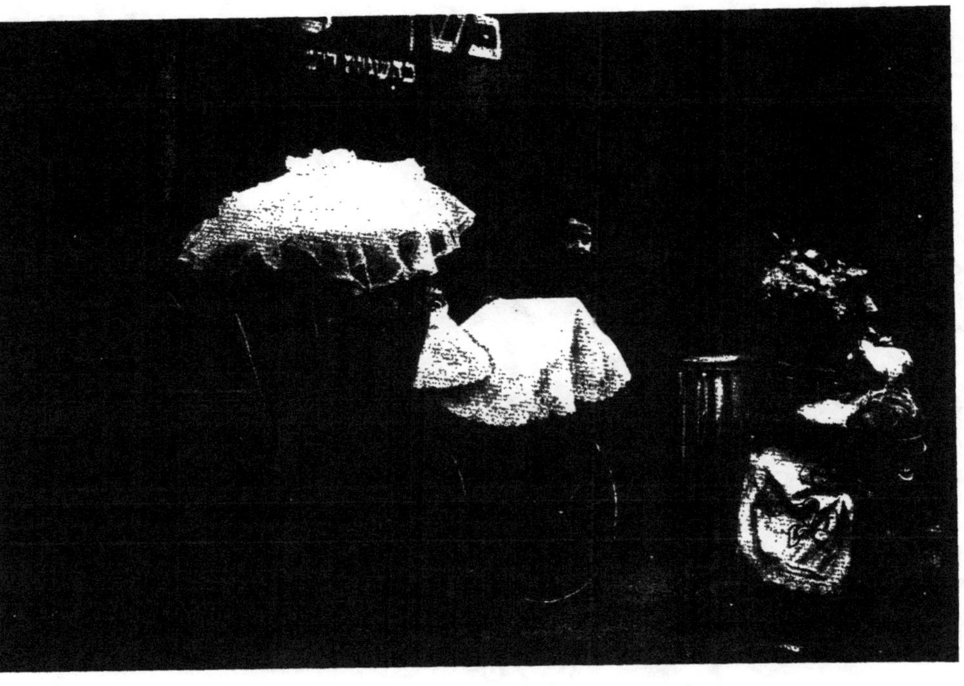

THE MORNING AIRING OF AN EAST SIDE HEIRESS.

The more intimately one comes into the home circle of the independent wage-earners the more clearly does the disadvantages of wealth stand revealed. Life must be lived so simply, the interests of life are so evident, that the value of words decreases; action expresses the heart perfectly. The very services the children render each other train them for the family life they will establish. The baby tended by an older brother and sister learns to depend on them for care, and that dependence in turn draws out a love and responsibility that could not have birth under any other conditions. The child who finds that in pain, weariness, suffering, a father and mother alone share its care; the elder children who see how naturally sacrifices are made for them, how little the father and mother value themselves, their ease, even their comfort, learn to value the love in the home and depend on it, give love to it, that money to buy service would bar out. The child who sees parents make sacrifices to enlarge his opportunities for education, seeing him as a positive factor in his own manhood, sees more than parental love in such sacrifices and stands in more than the relation of child to parents.

At the level where charity and dependence are large factors in the home life, the relation of parents to children is changed by their presence.

Art has given Charity the figure of a noble, benign woman, in the ample folds of whose garments children are protected. Too often in life she wears a short skirt, to make speed possible, suggesting in movements and voice the need of nervines, when she does not seem to have taken the bandage from the eyes of Justice for her own use, while neglecting to borrow her scales. Where Charity is the welcome guest, instinct is greater than intelligence in the parental relation. The home tie is slight; children become shrewdly self-dependent, physical hardships are more easily borne, and life is often a mere matter of shelter and food; the animal alone is kept alive. This represents a social level as remote from that of the independent wage-earner as is represented between the home's standards and requirements of a family living on fifteen hundred dollars a year and that of a family living on fifteen thousand dollars a year.

We use the word poor so carelessly that there is confusion where absolute misapprehension has not developed as to the character of the largest, most receptive, most responsive and most responsible class of citizens of New York. Politically they have been neglected, until the Citizens' Union gave them a formative part in political decisions. Here and there a score or more independent working men would be found in political organizations, because of an active political conscience, always hoping for better days, when the city would be given its imperative rights without regard to the State or national political complications. It was a hopeless fight, and has sent into the erratic political parties the majority of the independent working men now in them. The schemes of the politicians disgusted them, and new principals seemed to be the only hope for the clean-minded mind who did its own thinking.

The great mass of these independent, self-respecting, intelligent working-men voters were hunted for at election, but were not counted worthy to take a place in the councils of the politically active because they were feared. The Citizens' Union recognized their value and power, and they have come into their own as citizens. No greater service have the Settlements done the city than discovering this unused element in political power and centering it where it is recognized as the saving power in municipal government. These men stand at the head of the homes that reveal love—tender, protecting inspiring love—serving in unspoken unselfishness to the largest degree.

Thousands of mothers can testify to the cheerful sharing by fathers in the household burdens after a day of hard work; of cheerful going without necessities on the part of a father to give more than necessities to the children. Thousands of husbands and fathers will note the unselfishness and wisdom of a mother in caring for and enlarging the opportunities for the children, who are the common objects of love and ambition, and the confidence and love of the husband grows with the years. To the observer there is at the same time no more inspiring and depressing revelation than the parental love which asks nothing for itself, but all that life can give for the children, the visible expression of their mutual love. Often there is no thought given to a future of possible dependence. Wages do not make possible the care of the children at the standards of the parents, the buying of an environment that the experience of intelligent parents demands for them, and a bank account. The last is desirable, the first demand imperative. Faith is the anchor kept to be thrown out when the life currents are running toward the rocks of want and dependence. Nothing is kept back for personal use by these fathers and mothers. Sometimes this very unselfishness, when unregulated by wisdom, leaves them lonely and forsaken in old age. Those to whom they have given their lives have by the gift been placed in social positions that seemingly bar out the parents who made achievement possible. Even in the loneliness of old age the parents rejoice at the success and forget and forgive the separation. The end for which they worked has been attained, their children are successful, and they still count themselves nothing compared with their children.

It is the independent wage-earners who make the largest contributions to our wealth, commercial greatness, national prestige; yet the world, counting wealth by dollars, classifies these as poor. They are as far removed from the incapable, the degraded, the vicious, the dependent, the ignorant —who provide the themes for books—as far removed from the worthless, the deficient, the mentally, morally weak, so familiar to the people of wealth who give money or time, or both, to lessen their miseries, as they are in standard and ambition from the people counted wealthy. The cost of floor space on which to make a home may make them neighbors of the people who are the problems of a great city; they may live in regions that are the laboratory of the student of social and political conditions, but they live behind closed doors, bring up their children, so far as they can, uncontaminated by neighborhood evils, and overcome their environment to a surprising degree. There is no word to distinguish them from those who make capital of their poverty, and the world loses much because of the lack of a term that would express the class who are the hope of this nation, whose children are the promise of its established greatness.

The very limitations that small incomes impose on husbands and wives, strangers to social ambitions, bring into the relation an independence and *camaraderie* that possibilities of wealth would bar out. When a father and mother have one object in life, their children, they have no personal ambitions; their minds run in the same groove; they live of necessity a unit. When the aim is to give their children a better education than they had; to place them on a firmer foundation in the wage-earning world than the one on which the father and mother started; to save the children from the contaminating world as they had to meet it, there of necessity is a welded interest that bars out a world of distractions. The world in which such fathers and mothers live may seem narrow, but the smallness of the world makes the companionship the closer. As one gets into the inner circle of these homes, the small part that wealth plays in happiness is realized, and the comprehension of what constitutes essentials is gained. The man who knows the measure of his wage-earning power does not waste his nerve and vitality to earn more; the family grow to have fixed habits of expenditure, and content is attained that the social strugglers never know. The victim of nervous prostration is not found in the working-man's world; the fixed rate of wages relieves the nerves, but exercises the muscles and the balance of health is kept. The exceptions to this happy attainment are those whose mental or moral natures have not been adjusted to the happy, even life of the skilled, sober, industrious, thrifty working-man's family in New York.

The world of wealth would find itself rejected if it brought with it into the wage-earning world its moral standards, the rules of conduct are so simple in this world, the standards so elemental. An aldermanic candidate who in his own world is not counted ignorant, during the campaign of 1901 conceived the idea, which he had never held before, though this was the fourth time he had appealed to the suffrages of the people, that the women were a factor in political success. He decided to call on the wives, mothers and sisters of the voters in his district. It would be interesting to know his conclusions after his experience. He must have gained wisdom by his experiment, and heard some unwelcome truths. He announced to one of his hostesses that he thought if he called and showed himself they might see in him something that would persuade them that their husbands, fathers, brothers, or sons ought to vote for him. It would have been interesting to have seen his face when more than one hostess assured him that, having seen him, she felt bound to urge her husband to vote for the other candidate. Or when he was told by others that he must understand how certain he was of defeat, or he would not appeal to women. Still more interesting it would have been to see him when an outraged wife let down the flood-gates of her wrath because she blamed him for the periodic lapses from industry and sobriety of which her husband was guilty. The better class of voters of this candidate's party resented angrily the man calling on their wives. The root cause of the indignation of the men and women it was found was that this man dared to call when the husbands were not at home. In the world of work there is no place for social life in the day-time, and it argues ill for those who indulge in it. The Metropolitan Opera House in the evening would so shock the working man and his wife that they would never recover respect for those who frequent it. A high-necked lace dress with a low lining, worn in the evening by one from the other world to an East Side party, brought out this comment: "Oh! yes, she's all right. They all do it, the women; but isn't it awful?"

The moral standards for men and women in the world of work are the same. The immoral man is despised and avoided by the women. A woman who should maintain the smallest degree of friendship or acquaintance with a man known to be immoral would be avoided by her neighbors; she would be made to realize at once the cause of her offending.

A silly, pretty little woman, whose husband at times was cruel and brutal, ran away from him with another man. No one in the neighborhood could remember when such a thing had happened before, and the neighborhood resented it as a disgrace. The husband's brutality was well known; he was despised and ignored by the better element of men in the neighborhood. Had the wife gone alone, she would have had the support of a respectable minority, but now the husband was the object of deep sympathy. When the wife was found, and declared she would gladly starve with the partner of her disgrace—and there was a fair prospect at the time that she would—"than have the best in the land with my husband; he has kicked me out for the last time," she was cast out of the books of remembrance in that neighborhood. "She married him for better or worse," was the measure of a wife's duty among these wives and mothers.

The admiration of the explorer into this world of work and homes grows with the years for the people who make it, as indignation grows at the misunderstanding of its limitations, its possibilities, its beauty and greatness. For Matthew Arnold gave the true definition of greatness when he said it was the obstacles overcome, not his attainments, that made a man great. The explorer makes many discoveries—some that stimulate and surprise, some that puzzle and depress. The silence of love in this world is a revelation. Whether the terms of endearment are not in the language of this world, or whether the want of leisure and privacy stifle them, it is difficult to decide. Perhaps it is that the language of love is learned in a mother's arms; that when her service to her child must be physical, when it is but one of a thousand things demanding her care and thought—when her muscles must serve unceasingly—she has no time to express the love that strengthens them by words. It may be that the language of love does not grow within crowded walls, and that it is forced to express itself in service.

A man ranking high in the intellectual world once took for his theme, when preaching to a company of wage-earners and their wives, "Home Life." It was a rare inspiration that moved him

A BIT OF OLD GREENWICH.

to point out how much was lost to the home where the verbal expression of love was never heard. He said no higher inspiration to work his best could be given a man than his wife's good-bye kiss in the morning; nor a charm that would drive away care, worry and exhaustion more perfect than her welcoming kiss when he returned from his work at the close of the day. He pictured the feelings of the man who found his wife silent and unresponsive when he entered the house; who answered his query as to what was the matter with "Nothing." In his audience was a wife whose faithfulness and intelligence had made her husband far more than he could ever have been without her, a fact of which he was fully conscious; he was not allowed to forget it. This wife was deeply impressed by what she heard. She was ignorant because of lack of opportunity, untruthful because she was ignorant; she could not see the relations of things. Vindictive, because in her moral code you must resent any wrong, real or fancied, by an action that goes far deeper than that of the offender in its effect. Anything else would be an evidence of weakness. She expressed her contempt for one who would forgive an injury, and prided herself that she never did. She had enthusiasm, could inspire others, and proved herself as capable in leading them to do wrong as to do right. She was the power in her home, and established its standard of right and wrong that gave motive to the lives of her children. This night the speaker lifted the veil. There was something that belonged in the home that she alone could put there, and she had not. She resolved that she would part from and meet her husband with a kiss. It is best to let her tell her own story:

"I just made up my mind I'd do it." No girl of eighteen giving a confidence of a love affair could have shown more embarrassment than this mother of wage-earning children. "I did not know how I would do it, or what —— would say, but I just made up my mind I would kiss him when he came home. I thought about it all the next day. Late in the afternoon I made up my mind. Of course, I could not kiss him before the children. When it was most time for —— to come home, I sent them each on an errand that would keep them away until long after —— got home. I had the table all set and the supper cooking. At last I heard him come up the stairs. My land! How I trembled! I stood so that when the door opened he would not see me, and then I just kissed him before I had a chance to think. He staggered back, he was so surprised." She waited while an expression that should have been habitual changed her shrewd, hard face into a loving woman's. "But I never saw him look so happy," she continued. "I made up my mind I would kiss him every day when he came home. I could not kiss him in the morning, for the children were all there," she added decidedly; "but I can always send the little ones on errands at night."

Perhaps it was three weeks later that she told of the climax. "I had a toothache all day; I was tired and cross, for I had been washing. I stood by the fire, making the hash. Kittie was setting the table, when —— opened the door. I did not look up. He stood in the door a minute; then he asked, 'What's the matter, Jennie?' 'Nothing.' I knew I said it cross. I looked up then. —— looked so disappointed that I thought he'd cry. I just forgot the children, and right before them I kissed —— twice. I wish you could have seen his face. I burst out laughing when I looked at the two children. They stood staring at us with their mouths wide open. Do you know what I did? I kissed each of them. I don't believe I've kissed either since they were babies. I think they told the big ones in the front room when they came from work." This experiment in love-making did not continue. —— came home drunk one night, and for punishment the experiment was dropped and never resumed.

While it lasted, it had a most harmonizing effect on the whole family, and one wondered if it had been begun earlier, when the habit could have been easily fixed, what would have been the result.

The mother, from a worldly point of view, has been most successful. The children are in positions where skill is required, and wages seem to depend on health only. Yet they are not popular; are selfish and unsympathetic. They point to their own success as the reason why every family should succeed. The family has moved into new environment, establishing relations that have placed it several rounds higher than the level at which the home-making began; but it has no fixed place in the social world. The combined income of the five wages equals at times two thousand dollars a year.

Not every wife in this world of silent love is encouraged as this wife was. Another, a gentle, quiet woman, without children, thought she would try. "He sit so still when he came home. I bought a flower and put it on the table. I have what he like best for supper, and I wait. I listen over the banister. When he come near our flight, I slip back and wait in the room, leaving the door open so he can see. When he close the door I go up to him, put mine arms around his neck and kiss him. He take my arms, shove me back and say:

'What the matter mit you? You crazy?'" The woman was crying. The three friends sat silent a moment, and then one said: "You haf no children," and the wife nodded. That was her explanation, and theirs.

Perhaps no greater charm prevails in this world of wage-earners than the attitude toward motherhood. There will be found here and there the young woman who rebels against it, who may risk life rather than assume the care of a baby. When one goes back of this rebellion there is always found the influence of some older woman who has other ambitions, clothes, pleasure; who influences, or tries to influence, the young married women she meets; a woman who will even talk freely to girls against motherhood. There is in this world of workers the strong active public sentiment against childless women that more than counteracts this influence, and babies are welcomed when there is nothing but love to greet them, not much more to feed them or clothe them; but they are welcomed. The training of the children—natural, not acquired—to be fathers and mothers has doubtless a far-reaching effect in keeping this natural attitude of mind toward parenthood.

We get up a lot of wasted sentiment about the little mothers and fathers, not seeing that the offices are fitting them to meet a future when all that they learn in the care of baby brothers and sisters will make their lives easier as fathers and mothers. Often the only opportunity they have for expressing affection is the little baby given to their care.

How well one must know this part of the wage-earning world before it is possible to appreciate the fact that the boy is being trained by "his baby" for that future when he will share with the mother of his child its care. It is a constant revelation to find how intelligent the young men at this level are about children, and how frankly and unconsciously they will express it and condemn the ignorant or careless treatment of a child. The relation of the wage-earning children to the little children is paternal often. The little ones know that the elder ones work and care for them, and they render an obedience that is often amusing. With sisters this takes another form. If the elder girl has ideas and tastes, especially if she has skill, she will often entirely decide how the younger children shall dress; often the younger children would not be at all satisfied with clothes the elder girls did not select and design. Here again will be found a half-maternal attitude that secures obedience and regulates privileges; that sometimes ignores the rightful authority in the home. The

A LITTLE FATHER.

young girl who has an elder sister working and secures work with her is considered very fortunate. Two sisters are known, now past middle life. One is quite a handsome woman, the other plain. The handsome sister is the younger; she never, when she was a wage-earner, went through the streets alone. The elder sister, when they did not work together, escorted the younger one back and forth to her work. Now, the mother of three children, nothing could persuade her to go on the streets alone beyond the corner store. Her husband, in a city department on a small salary, always attends her in shopping expeditions, and all social engagements are made with respect to his hours of freedom. She receives a wealth of love, and tenderness, and protection. Selfish? Yes, till one wonders at the blindness of those who do her homage.

Once a very sensible wife and mother, whose intelligence and devotion are raising the family many degrees above that of the generation preceding her and her husband, said: "I shall watch my children. My mother let one of my sisters exact far more than her share of wages. She coaxed or cried, or both, until she got what she wanted. The rest of us gave in, because we would not worry mother; you see that, now we are all married, she expects us to save her from worry and work; we have to; she cannot get along." In a moment she continued: "Haven't you seen it, that in every large family there is one who gets more and gives less than the others?" A statement profoundly true, but not confined to any one social level.

Among the discoveries the explorer into this world makes is that life is full of compensations. One learns to overlook bad housekeeping, when it is discovered that a cross, impatient word is never spoken by the house-mother; that the children are the companions of the mother; that no one else is so attractive; that she is never too busy to listen to anything that interests them. One learns to forgive the needlessly shabby dressing of children, when it is discovered that they are well nourished and cared for, and that the husband and father never fails to declare that his wife is the best cook in the city and always has his meals on time. Usually this mother is fat, full of fun, and laughs as though tears were not in the world.

Order, cleanliness and economy do not appeal as cardinal virtues when it is found that there is no room for the children in the house, no money to buy them the smallest pleasure where these over-estimated virtues predominate. It is found usually that the worry of maintaining standards that ignore the rights of the family, and to which they have been sacrificed, have seared the mother's head and heart, and she no longer responds to the maternal emotions; she becomes the victim of her own habits and cannot reform. Perhaps it is this type of woman who creates the most barren home; the one that is quite as prolific a source of supply to the saloons and the streets as that of the degenerate housekeeper out of whose life spiritual impulse has departed, and into which ideals and ambitions were never born.

It is difficult at times to decide whether to laugh at or resent the criticisms one often hears of the extravagances of the poor. When one becomes familiar with the demands for rent, coal, shoes, for clothes that must be worn to work and school; for the things the cost of which cannot be put below a certain sum—food always can be regulated—and compares these fixed charges with the income available, the management of money in the independent working man's family amounts to genius, and it must take generations of economists to produce it.

Unfortunately, in New York emphasis is laid on clothes. Extravagance in dress is the habit of the city. The people seen in the streets, in the stores, in public conveyances, show a singular uniformity in clothes; this is as true of men as of women. The differences are in manners and English. The spirit of the land is as yet materialistic, and the democratic spirit shows itself in the outward forms. The tailor-made gown was not looked upon as a regenerator of æsthetic standards, but it has proved that. Its simplicity and durability has released money that formerly was used in useless trimming. The ready-trimmed hat is also a lever in throwing the scale in the right direction.

The attention to school decoration of recent years has given new standards for the home. The wage-earning world grows more harmonious in its demands on wages; the home now makes its demands for decoration that the workers obey. Signs outside of tenement houses renting suites of four rooms for twenty and twenty-five dollars per month announce: "Burlaped halls; parlors in white and blue;" or, "Tiled halls, open gas grates, fancy chandeliers." The men who hire these apartments earn from fifteen to twenty-five dollars a week or more. Thousands of American working men pay these rentals to save their children from the environment inseparable from the surroundings that must be endured if a fair proportion of their wages were used for rent. One grows to reverence the courage that enables a husband and wife, with only one pair of hands earning the home needs, to assume such rents. No higher evidence of the manhood and righteous ambition of the American citizen could be given than this: that he places his all to secure for his children a home that is reasonably protected; that offers opportunities for cleanliness and privacy. Renting a room to a lodger will sometimes make less demands on a father's wages for rent; sometimes the rent is assumed in the hope of securing lodgers, and then the struggle is pathetic, but borne because the children must not grow up in a less desirable neighborhood. If one were asked for the standard by which to measure the civilization of each family in the wage-earning world, the reply would have to be, "Rent." It at once makes the most and the least return; it is the tyrant which makes or mars the home life. When a family of eight, having a combined income of thirty-six dollars a week, are content to live in three rooms, one knows about what to expect in social standards, and how many generations it will take to raise the home level. When a family of six—five wage-earners—who began life at almost the homeless level, gradually come into a combined income of two thousand dollars a year, it is not to be expected that its standards of needs will be those of a college graduate on the same income. Often no member of the family can read readily. School life was, especially for the elder children, an intermittent one, and truth did not regulate the beginning of wage-earning of any of the children. The younger children probably warred against school long before fourteen years of life gave them freedom. There is natural intelligence, a certain manner acquired through observation, but no standard of intellectual life. Their very intelligence makes such families conscious of their shortcomings, and it is this consciousness that leads to the aggressiveness of manner that is so offensive, so often mistakenly called the American manner. It is the manner that is due to awakened consciousness which in the next generation will know when to wear evening dress, if not how.

The use of money in such families is for show. It would be counted extravagant to buy a book, or a ticket to an oratorio or a concert to hear the best music. It would in such a family be counted useless to train the younger children to wage-earning by education. The heads of the family will be hospitable where it counts as showing how much more they have than the others in their world. They receive from their world what snobbishness receives everywhere. Snobbishness, on the whole, is not common even where the income would remove the family from a tene-

A CORNER IN OLD GREENWICH.

ment-house environment. The uncertainty of work, and the absolute dependence of the worker on wages, make snobbishness dangerous; that often proves a boomerang their observation shows.

The spirit of helpfulness may not find so free a field of operations when wages are two dollars and a half and over a day, but it is in readiness. Sickness in a neighbor's family will show that it has not been lost because of prosperity, but it is less lavish; there is dawning consciousness that self-preservation is the first law of nature; that home has the first right to strength and thought; that only the surplus is available for the world of friends. The same thriftlessness which makes a family accept charity without question is the cause of their generosity. As the sense of responsibility develops, the observer discovers a reserve in the giving of either their money or their strength to those about them; kindness abounds, but generosity is regulated as one goes up the scale in the world of wage-earners. Not only that, but in the direst need the needy, as one goes up the scale, regulate the degree of freedom given the closest friends. It often borders on the tragic, the suffering borne in silence, and revealed often when the time for help is passed.

This division of the people into rich and poor without gradations and without a comprehension of the standards and needs that make new worlds up and down the scale, has had a serious effect on the home life, the church life of the people, the political life of the people. The churches have driven out the very people in the tenement-house regions who needed them and whom they needed.

Corrupt administration has imposed burdens on the homes which for a time the voters in turn felt powerless to lift. The independent wage-earner found his hope of political recognition in allegiance to the political machines. The leaders, his inferiors often mentally, and still more surely morally, were at least approachable and familiar, and the man who made his own life found too often that only in the political circle of interest was he the equal of those who led. Here there was no manner that expressed condescension or superiority. His own language was spoken; he was at home. That these men allowed themselves to be used was the natural result of the habit of indifference to the real issues in a municipal campaign so common in New York. When the burdens of a corrupt administration pressed on the homes; when the leaders for righteous government acknowledged by appealing to the makers of this country, the plain people, that they were an integral part of the city's government, they responded, and by their response overthrew the corrupt government that the indifference of all classes had helped to make powerful.

The century opens well. Capitalist and wage-earner sit at the same board, having equal voice in the plans for redeeming the city from partisan machine control.

As one thinks of the change, one sees that the evils that disgraced New York were due to the indifference of the millionaires and the honest working men. It is the response of the political conscience of both to the need of the city that has been its redemption; its only sure protection is the activity of that conscience three hundred and sixty-five days of each year in all the years to come.

CHAPTER X.

WHERE LIES THE RESPONSIBILITY?

It took years for the evils of political machines to make life unbearable in New York. Not until the tremendous evils it imposed on child-life were given emphasis did the public sentiment of the city find intelligent expression—voice the moral conscience of the whole people. That dishonest administration of the city government imposed burdens on the home of the poor man no intelligent person disputed; but few knew how heavy the burdens or how far-reaching the effects on character. The people who suffered most were, in the very nature of things, the ones who could not see these influences, or estimate truly the degrading effect on character. The people who resented the conditions that made life harder in the tenements; who resented the environment which made the bringing up of children in innocence, integrity, and decency often impossible, were those who were in the minority. Hopelessness of overcoming the evils made some voters the forgers of their own chains.

Newspapers gave columns to the exposure of

the evils of the political methods which made individuals rich at the cost of the homes of the city, especially the homes of the poor. But the phase of this influence that was most degrading could only be learned by living in the regions, one of the people, suffering with them the burdens dishonesty imposed.

When college-trained men and women established their homes in the regions of the tenements, making friends with the people, associating freely with them, especially with the young people and the children, they discovered that the worst evil with which the people were contending was the constant lowering of the moral standards due to the influence of the political organization that seemed to regulate even the right of the people to earn a living. It was but a step from fear to favor; but a little time before the man outweighed the principle; Justice became the handmaid of "pull," and the people living wholly under the environment corrupt political power created, knew no government but that of the "leader" and the man who represented him. To trade votes was no disgrace, for it meant a share in the perquisites that political power held. These men and women of trained intelligence saw that the corrupting of the moral standards of the people was a far greater evil—an evil that was of far greater moment to the whole people than the maladministrations that affected their physical being, though it led to death.

It was the revelations the Settlement workers were able to make to a half-informed community of wealth and trained intelligence that led to the redeeming of the city. It made the active combination of wealth and poverty that brought into the political arena the dormant consciences that created in 1901 the Apotheosis, New York redeemed, that is the justification of democracy to the world.

The iniquity, ignorance and indifference that create and maintain a system of municipal administration based on the theory that politics is a profession, and each promoter the architect of his own fortune, to be built at the expense of the citizens, is the reflection of the character of the citizens. The system is never the product of one man's brains, nor does its growth ever begin at the top. It begins always in the smallest political unit, where the man who wishes the office in the gift of that unit stands closest to the people. The bargaining for votes begins there. The number of exchanges of votes for favors and places successfully accomplished makes the "boss," the man who represents law and order; who is judge, and jury, and keeper of the jail to those who do his bidding. As the political units develop their bosses—"leaders," in voters' parlance—the system grows until the chain is complete, and each political henchman, in the order of his importance, takes his share of the people's money. The perquisites reach millions before the thousands are distributed that enables the leader to pose as the all-pervading friend to the district in time of need.

The political units where this system of government in the interest of the "boss" have their strongest hold are the best evidences of the moral degeneracy that follows. Here the liquor saloons flourish, the headquarters of the "leader" and his cohorts, used in the order of rank in the system, from the gayly lighted, silver-bedecked, mirror-lined bar-room to the smoky, dirty, vilely kept den where those gather who have no use in life but to vote according to orders and work for the political leader's entrenchment. These saloons represent the primary school and the university of the voters of the district. They represent all the educational and recreative opportunity of most of the adults. They establish the habits of thinking for the majority of the people, for they are the lyceum where all questions are discussed that interest the people. The most interesting is how to get wages, as it is the most important. The common struggle creates common bonds of sympathy. All principles go down before the concrete, understandable fact that if the "boss" is beaten, work will cease for neighbor, friend, and friend's friend. Each man learns through every course in this training school of citizens that the paramount duty of each voter is to keep the "boss" in power. It means wages, or the hope of wages, under the least strenuous of employers, the city. Men work hard for the system, not because the moral nature of many of them is not in revolt against the system, but because the keeping of a home for wife and children is at stake. Often the voter's necessities, his ignorance often, his rebellion against wealth often, his unrest, undermine his moral nature, blind his intelligence, and he forges the chains that bind him in slavery to a system that will cast him aside, and refuse him a reason when there is no use for him. The voter may work during an election campaign half knowing that to secure another worker in the interests of the political system the place he holds has been promised to another after election. This fear and this hope enters the homes; women and children are educated under the moral degradation that enslaves husbands, sons, brothers, friends, lovers. The standards of morals are established even in childhood by the working of the systems of political

TAKING THEIR TURN IN THE YARD AT THE SETTLEMENT.

machines. There is one measure of morals, *success*. What succeeds is right.

A small house was hired, through the generosity of several women, for the purpose of providing a place for recreation and social opportunity for a number of Christians—that is, people not Hebrews—left in a thickly settled Hebrew district. These Christians, a mere remnant, resented the opportunities offered the Hebrews, and while they might have availed themselves of them, they would not, so strong was the race prejudice. Shortly after the house was opened a delegation of boys appeared asking for the use of the large room for a boys' club. The privilege was given on the conditions that one of the workers interested in the house should have the privilege of visiting the room freely when the club was in session; that the club should pay twenty cents per month for the use of the room; that it should be limited to twenty members for three months. Before the first month had passed, it was decided that unless the club would accept a director, it was a waste of the space and light to let these boys use the room. They called themselves a debating and literary club. They knew nothing of literature naturally and less of debating. They were told that they must accept a director, a man who would instruct them in parliamentary law, guide them in debate and suggest subjects for study, or they must give up the room. They were very angry, but finally decided to accept the director. Their constitution provided for an election every month, a provision which kept them in a turmoil all the time. When the majority were convinced of this, and voted that officers should be elected every three months, the dissenting minority withdrew to form a new club, to meet somewhere else. Two weeks later, on club night, the bell rang. The leader of the minority, who had been elected president of the new club, asked if they might come back. They did not like the place where they met. After a conference with the original club, it was decided that, if they chose to come back as members of the club and pay their dues—three cents per week—they might come back. The conditions were accepted, and the seceding minority were to be reinstated as members of the original club on the next meeting night. As the petitioner was leaving, he turned innocently to the director and said: "Say, we've elected a couple of new fellows. They can come in, can't they?" The club consented conditionally on the "new fellows" being peaceable. The next meeting night came. The bell rang. In order to do full honor to the returning prodigals, the president went to the door. There was a rush and a scramble; the eight boys who withdrew, followed by twenty-two others, crowded into the room and demanded an election at once. They declared they were in the majority now, and had a right to the presidency for one of their own number. It was impossible to eject them, had it been wise. The question was postponed for one week and an arbitrator selected.

When the next meeting night came, some of the new recruits had dropped out and their places had been taken by older boys. The original members, who had maintained the club, were told to sit together and keep absolutely quiet. The constitution declared that no boy was a member of the club who did not pay an initiation fee of five cents; this included the first month's dues. The first strange boy was asked: "Have you paid your initiation fee?" The leader, a boy not fourteen, sprang forward and pressed a five-cent piece in the boy's hand, saying: "Pay it now. Joe's the treasurer." The cue had been given him, and he proceeded to give out nickels to the new boys, urging them to "pay Joe quick." During this scene another of the receding minority took his position in front of the door to prevent any boy leaving the room with the money. The performance was stopped; the opulent small boy, who it was evident was buying votes for the presidency, was told to gather up his nickels. The recruits were told, after an explanation, why they must leave, and to their credit be it recorded some of them resented the position in which they had been placed and promised the misleading leader an unhappy next day before they left. It was then decided that the twelve members who had constituted the majority should ballot individually for the eight who had seceded, as though they had never belonged to the club. It is unnecessary to say that the boy who made the trouble was rejected. Not one of those boys was fifteen years old, yet they had learned and understood the method of the political organizations of the region. Their elders, those they loved, used these methods, and succeeded by them in getting place and power. The man who succeeded in sharp practice in politics was the "boss." The man who was beaten was not smart. The measure of morals was success, not methods used to attain that success.

A woman's club, organized several years before, used this house. The husbands of several of them organized a men's club, and met in the house one evening in the week. Several of those men were affiliated with the political organizations of the district; some held positions under the city government through these affiliations.

When the Citizens' Union campaign began in 1897, the women who established the house offered it and the yard for one evening a week to the Citizens' Union Campaign Committee. Illustrated lectures were given to the people of the neighborhood, the friends of the clubs using the house, and the parents of children in the children's clubs. This declared the sentiments of the women who established the house, which were emphasized when a picture of the Citizens' Union candidate for Mayor was put in the window. It became evident at once that there was trouble in the women's club; some of the members of the men's club never entered the house after the picture was placed. The Citizens' Union was defeated. At once the friction in the women's club developed, till it seemed wise to disband it. It was announced that the house had been given up, and that all the work done there must be placed elsewhere. The younger clubs were housed in the Clark Memorial. The women's club, in spite of the friction, voted to keep together, and, with the City History Club, asked to be received at the College Settlement, which generously, and at great inconvenience, arranged to receive them. The members of the women's club, numbering forty-five, voted unanimously to become identified with the College Settlement work, and pledged themselves to that work. The one woman who had resisted this decision in secret stood with the rest pledged to the Settlement. At once she incited trouble at the Settlement. She was voted out of the club. When the decision was announced, she, with the treasurer of the club and three others, walked out of the house, the treasurer taking the club treasurer's book and the money, over seventeen dollars. Sunday's papers announced the incorporation of a club under the old name. The incorporators were the five women who had left the club at the Settlement. The business of incorporating was attended to by a political leader in the State Assembly. One of these women had held a position in a city department, secured for her by a leader of one of the political parties; one was the wife of a man holding a city position through active affiliation with the other political party; another was the wife of a man who was striving for prominence in political affairs in the district, irrespective of party; the other was shrewd, ambitious, vindictive. The club before this break had done charitable work; had helped families who needed help, through the generosity of friends of wealth. It had a limited membership, and election was the assurance of certain qualities in the woman who was received as a member. All this had commanded attention and could furnish political capital. To hold this for one or the other of the political parties was the intention of the women who incorporated under the club name and persuaded six of the club members to join them.

The treasurer was so evidently the cat's-paw of those who were managing the affair that, while steps were being taken to punish her for taking the money, the club at the Settlement voted not to prosecute her, because it would be a stigma on her as long as she lived, because she would have to stand with women arrested for drunkenness and disorderly characters in the dock. The original club remained at the Settlement. The minority who withdrew, a total of eleven, began active and aggressive work. They hired the use of a working-girls' club-room. They began to work according to the most approved methods of political leaders. They attended the outings of a political association; tried to do what they called charitable work, but which this very group proved they could not do justly while in the little house.

The Fusion campaign of 1901 brought unexpected complications to the club woman. The Tammany influence was stronger than the Republican, and the women who had led in the incorporating of the club withdrew. Unfortunately, the opportunity to give this whole group a strong lesson in morals was lost, and they have been accepted where, had the genesis of their club been understood, it is but reasonable to suppose they would have had no moral support, and for that reason would have gained a moral lesson.

The training most needed by the people of narrow experience and limited intelligence is that of clear distinctions between right and wrong by those they class above themselves. That shrewdness is not a moral virtue; that revenge is mean and not the function of mortals, is the one lesson intelligence and moral standards can teach convincingly.

Recently it was the privilege of the writer to visit a Parents' Society connected with a school in the outskirts of Brooklyn. The spirit of good fellowship that existed, not only among the teachers of the school, but between the teachers and the parents, was a revelation. That there was a unifying cause was certain. What was it? One of the mothers, during a walk to the station, revealed it. In response to a comment on the good feeling so evident, the mother replied: "Yes, I feel it. Mr. ——," naming a member of the Board of Education, "at prayer meeting the other night spoke of the school and what a power it was in this part of the city. We owe it all to him. He's done everything he could do for the school, and he has made all the ministers and the priests friends of the school." She was quiet a minute, and then added: "Years ago, when he first began fighting for the school, people used to call him a 'boss.' I think that kind of a boss would be good in every school. I tell my husband we ought to be glad that we bought that lot out here and built when we did, for we helped to make Mr. —— successful. If leading men to do your will means being a 'boss,' Mr. —— is one. But the city needs hundreds of such 'bosses.'" The man is a simple American citizen, bearing a foreign name, who saw clearly there were more ways of serving and saving his country than by carrying a rifle.

In the last analysis the "boss" as he is in New York to-day is the product of many roots. The one that goes deepest in the soil, the course of his deepest hold, can be traced to the doors of our churches. The men who have failed to see that they owed an allegiance to the city that does not differ in degree from what they owed the Church; the men who failed to see that the Church was a positive factor in civic life; that its effectiveness in the community was dependent on the standards it demanded and helped to maintain in the city; that on it rested the responsibility for civic character-building—on these men rest the heaviest responsibility for the evolution of the political "boss" and the evils of which he is the personification.

Men and women give money to maintain church services in sections where political corruption and civic neglect have resulted in creating an environment that makes decent living impossible; an environment that has so degenerating an influence that the people become a factor in the problem it presents, for they have sunk to its level.

In those sections the tools of the "boss," his active political agents, use the most despicable methods. The tool of the principal is valuable as he is conscienceless. His crumbs are the minor offices in the gift of the people; the lesser tools get "jobs," which the very limitations of their minds make them believe they must use to secure the largest return of money and power to themselves —a conception largely due to the indifference of the men who willingly delegate their civic responsibilities. Every man and woman who pays the slightest attention to the conditions under which the poor are forced to live, know that these conditions are responsible for the existence of nine-tenths of the eleemosynary institutions, private and public. They know that many of these institutions, could they stand before the community in their true character, would be recognized as disgraceful blots upon our civilization. They exist because so many good people in the community have found greater pleasure in establishing and maintaining them than in working actively to prevent the growth of the conditions that peoples them.

Again and again one sees the names of men and women working actively on these boards of mangement who would not give a moment's thought to a meeting called in the interests of better civilization in sections of the city where their own homes are located; who know nothing of the conditions of the schools, the streets, the tenement houses, the factories, or the administration of the law in regard to them. There are men who would resent the charge of ignorance who do not know the names of the officers they either actively or passively elected to office in the political unit in which are their homes. They do not attend the primaries, defending their absence on the ground that they could accomplish nothing by their presence—a defense that is in itself a self-accusation. If their divine right of citizenship has been forfeited, it is by their own civic sin of omission. The longer one studies the evils that have grown up in the administration of the business of the great municipality of New York, the clearer one sees that the sins of omission are responsible for their growth—far more responsible than the sins of commission against which intelligent voters rail, when they do not use them as salve for their political consciences. It is a profound truth that in a republic the character of the people is shown in the character of the men the people elect to office. This is as true of the ward as of the nation.

The political units of government in New York are, in the main, inhabited by the rich and poor, the intelligent and the ignorant; those who can reason from effect to cause, and those who cannot reason at all. Yet in these sections the worst possible home conditions will exist—unsanitary schools, dirty streets, badly paved. Saloons will abound and political corruption will go unheeded. Why? Because no men of intelligence and responsibility will accept the minor offices that mean the administration of the affairs of this unit in the interest and for the protection of the whole people.

When men of position in the professional and business world signify their willingness to accept the least office in the gift of the people, the daily papers announce the fact in large headlines, and the men become marked as capable of great self-sacrifice, they become preëminent for the time. The men who have controlled the nominations, those who have no other visible means of support than these minor offices and political patronage, resent the suggestion of men of professional and financial fortunes accepting these offices; they consider the appearance of a man holding business or professional positions of power or influence as a candidate for a minor office as an invasion, an intrusion of their personal rights; it is an attempt to defraud them. They do not hesitate to publicly claim the right to nomination and election as the reward for their activity in politics. And they do this when they cannot point to one thing done officially to justify their claims to the suffrages of the people. They dare to do it in the face of the knowledge, held by the people, that they use their offices often for personal ends, defrauding the people.

The scores of voters who have places within the patronage of a minor official see the danger to them of an official who would place merit in advance of votes. The man of position may be far from wealthy; may consent to serve the city at a financial loss; but the active voters live so remote from the voters at the top that the election is almost certain to be decided on class lines; and the defeat of the non-professional politician is accepted by every man, woman and child in the poorer portion of the district as a personal triumph; the evidence that the poor man has friends to back him in his fight for place and power; that the poor must work together politically.

Whose fault is it? The good, intelligent, responsible citizens who delegated the government of their city to the men who use it for their personal gain. The good men in active politics, who openly concede the right to the minor offices in the city government to men whom they know are ignorant, and not infrequently know equally well are dishonest, and who will sacrifice the interest of the people to strengthen the system that means personal gains.

The political conditions of the city several years ago gave birth to one of the periodic moral upheavals that resulted in the election of a strong, earnest, loyal, church-supporting citizen as Mayor. This Mayor was anxious to raise the character of the city government. He determined to accomplish this by the character of his appointments. He had more than a superficial knowledge of the public schools, which at that time were the theater for the exercise of political "pulls." It was known for years that the Board of Education had been used to a greater or less extent to pay political debts, to create political capital for future use by some of its most active members. The new Mayor had it in his power to change the character of the Board, and he carefully considered his appointments.

In one of the sections of the city where, numerically as to families, wealth and poverty were fairly balanced, a section having in it churches of every denomination, many of them maintaining missions in the same political unit—there was at least this expression of neighborly interest—the schools were among the first built in the city. The last school building erected at the time of this Mayor's election had been built twenty years before; one had been built when the foundation for the pillars of the elevated road had been set in front of the site before it was purchased by the Board of Education, and was now in the heart of a crowded foreign settlement, had no out-door playground; the third building in the school district was so old, so badly planned, that for years effort had been made to secure a new building, but were defeated by the indifference, and at times the opposition, of the best citizens of the district, according to their own estimate.

The new Mayor determined to put the best men in the district on the Board. Twenty-eight men in that district, men of power, men of standards, some of them philanthropists actively interested in work for the poor, declined. The men appointed, the best he could get to serve, were unfit for the position—mentally unfit, for they were uneducated; or morally unfit, because any position paid or unpaid under the city government was conceived by them as just so great an opportunity to create political capital or realize perquisites put within their control by their appointments. The Mayor had begun at the top to make his appointments. The declinations of the honor were because of lack of time, a lack of knowledge. When the appointments were announced, there was a storm of criticism, and none more violent than the majority of the men who declined to serve on the Board.

At this time there was a great deal of activity among many leading women in the State to have a bill passed by the Legislature that would compel the Mayor of cities of the first class to appoint women in the proportion of one-third of the whole number appointed to the Boards of Education of those cities. The greatest activity for this measure was exercised in Brooklyn. One of the leaders, when asked a question about one of the schools in her own district, did not know where the school was. She had been a tax-payer in the district twenty-two years, and was considered a progressive woman. Her chief reason for working for this bill, for spending money freely in the interest of its success, was man's indifference to school matters. Perhaps if the command, "Feed my lambs" had been given to Dorcas instead of Peter, she might have developed enough sense of responsibility about the mental food given to know where the school buildings of her own school district were located.

In this school district, October, 1901, there were 574 children on half-day classes. There was no manual training, though the pupils in the schools were, for the most part, the children of day laborers, mechanics, and clerks on small salaries. There was no free library, nor prospect of any, because public sentiment did not demand it. There was one small park, difficult of access. To reach it from the outer sections of the district, the tracks used by nine lines of trolley cars must be crossed. There were no public baths, except one in summer, near the mouth of a large sewer. One of the schools had no out-door playground; two had the closets in the in-door play-grounds. There was no room where the teachers could retire if ill, or where they could take their luncheons; no rooms where pupils could be privately interviewed or taken if ill. Yet it is in this very district, where the oldest and wealthiest families of the city live; where nine-tenths of the philanthropic enterprises of the city have been born, and where the moral upheavals for the regeneration of the city will always find their quota of leaders, that there is developing some of the worst evils of a cosmopolitan city. Within its borders is a fair-sized Italian city, with scores of sweat-shops. Across the thoroughfare is a large Irish village lying at the foot of the hill, the streets dirty, unpaved, the houses in an unsanitary condition. Some of them are overrun with rats of enormous size. The streets at the top of the hill are beginning to yield to the pressure of the crowds at the foot. Specific houses seem to have in them the very germs of immorality and degeneracy. Women who have made a struggle when, by misfortune, forced to move into these houses cease to struggle, and yield to the influences about them. The tenement-house laws are violated openly.

There are not less than six missions, with twice that number of churches, in this one section; but so far as the environment of the poor is concerned, they might as well not exist. The majority of the tax-payers, those who command public respect and confidence, will not serve authoritatively in the political unit in which are their homes, in which their children must grow up. They will not take offices that would put it in their power to change the environment of the homes of the poor by securing the rights, enforcing the laws, that would protect all of the homes from the evils of vice, ignorance and unsanitary conditions. But these men when wealthy will support liberally institutions made necessary by their civic indifference.

No man in a pulpit in the section has ever made a study of it to arouse the conscience and energies of the members of his church to their political duties. Unfortunately the women, for the most part, are as ignorant of the condition, and as indifferent. Because of the unsanitary conditions of the houses occupied by the poor, the dirty streets, the restrictions of child life, the lack of opportunity for moral development, the total dearth of recreative opportunity for the boys and girls, the young men and women who are wage-earners, the lack of educational facilities for the children who must be educated, if at all, at the expense of the State, the section is a prolific source of supply to the institutions the intelligent, sympathetic, wealthy women of the section are so active in creating and sustaining.

The indifference of the wealthy and responsible to the conditions prevailing in parts of this section is so well known that officers at the heads of the city department ignore complaints, or treat them as incidents to be tolerated as part of the experiences of their official life.

The penalty is being paid in the steady decline

of real estate values, the gradual spread of the undesirable part of the community, the exodus of the wealthiest to the sections more remote from the tenements.

The environment that has a degenerating influence on the people of limited means in that section is not due primarily to the political corruption of those using their positions to secure their own ends, but to the criminal attitude of the men in the churches and intelligent men not in them, who refuse to assume the political responsibilities that are their birthrights; the criminal indifference of those who fail to know the necessities of which the homes of the poor whom God gave into their charge stand in need. This section of the city is typical, not peculiar. Every section of New York gives evidence of the divorce between the churches and the political control that makes the environment of the home and the churches.

The city is what the good, active people of the city want it to be—no better, no worse. The condition of the most uncared-for section gives the church's answer to the question, "Am I my brother's keeper?" The mark of Cain may not be visible, but every child who goes out of life because its right to light, air, sunshine has not been protected is a charge against the Church. Every boy and girl whose life record is shadowed, blackened because their right to education, to training, to freedom to develop physically, mentally, morally, spiritually was denied them through political indifference, are the evidences of the failure of the churches to live up to the light which Christ left to their keeping. His followers do not march through the cities of the poor, an army.

When Christ said, "The second is like unto it, love thy neighbor as thyself," He did not not mean the ethical conception for which the Church has stood, but the broad, Christ-like conception of brotherhood which would protect "thy neighbor" from the evils of his own ignorance and weakness; that would use one's best strength in his interest seven days in the week.

www.ingramcontent.com/pod-product-compliance
Lightning Source LLC
LaVergne TN
LVHW020603110826
845149LV00002B/358